DRIVING THE LIGHT HORSE

DRIVING THE LIGHT HORSE

TRAINING FOR PLEASURE AND COMPETITION

Charlene Roth

PRENTICE
HALL PRESS
EQUESTRIAN
BOOKS

PRENTICE HALL PRESS
New York   London   Toronto   Sydney   Tokyo

dedicated with affection and respect
to
Jane A. Patterson

Prentice Hall Press
15 Columbus Circle
New York, New York 10023

Published in 1988 by the Prentice Hall Trade Division

PRENTICE HALL PRESS and colophon are registered
trademarks of Simon & Schuster Inc.

Originally published by Arco Publishing, Inc.

Illustrations by Charlene Roth
Photographs by Jerry and Katie Miller except where indicated
otherwise

Library of Congress Cataloging in Publication Data

Roth, Charlene Davis, 1945–
    Driving the light horse.
    Includes index.
    1. Driving of horse-drawn vehicles.   I. Title.
SF305.R78   1984   798'.6   83-25667
ISBN 0-668-05652-5 (Cloth Edition)

Manufactured in the United States of America

10 9 8 7 6 5 4 3

First Prentice Hall Press Edition

CONTENTS

ACKNOWLEDGMENTS

I would like to thank the many people who helped me compile the information for the following book; specifically Jerry and Katie Miller who painstakingly took many of the photographs; *The Driving Digest Magazine*, who supplied photographs of the 1982 World Driving Championships; Mr. Williamson of Weston Manor who put me in contact with Major Coombs and Ian Brooke; Major T. Coombs who kindly sent me notes from England; Ian Brooke, who supplied many of the photographs of British drivers; Tom Ryder, who read the finished manuscript; and the many individuals who lent me photographs of their horses for inclusion in the book.

INTRODUCTION

Driving horses in harness is an ancient practice. It is believed that primitive peoples drove the horses they domesticated long before they rode them. Probably the animals were too small to carry a rider with ease and the people had not yet developed the requisite equipment and skills. Most likely the horse was tied with a crude rawhide harness to wheelless travois or sledges. Initially horses were led. Wild ass and oxen are known to have served in this manner in some areas of the world before the horse was domesticated. It would have been logical to use the newly tamed horse in the same capacity. Artifacts, pictorial representations, folklore, and some archeological theory support this supposition.

The history of the wheel is closely connected to the growth of driving. Its evolution is believed to have been a natural and necessary part of the success of agricultural peoples. The invention of the wheel can be pinpointed to western Asia during prehistoric times. It spread from there to the Mediterranean region and finally to Africa, but it wasn't until the Bronze Age that use of the wheel became widespread. Early wheels were heavy, solid disks with a hole cut in the center through which an axle passed. The wheels were held in place with wooden pegs or pins. Eventually sections were cut out between the rim and the axle to make wheels lighter and more decorative, but it was many centuries before spokes made an appearance. Spoked wheels began to replace solid wheels around 2000 B.C. In the beginning they had four spokes. Six- and eight-spoke wheels were in use by 1000 B.C. The size of the wheels was determined by terrain. The Chinese developed enormous wheels to handle marshy and sandy footing. Smaller wheels were practical on the hard, rocky ground common to Mesopotamia. Primitive wheels were bound with leather, although as soon as technology allowed, a metal shoe or rim was fitted around the wood.

Evidence that horses were used in China and the Middle East at about the same time suggests to many historians that several widely separated groups simultaneously discovered the unique attributes of the horse as a beast of burden. What seems to be earliest tangible evidence of driving horses was discovered in China, where remnants of chariots were found beside symbolic depictions of horses which date to 3500 B.C. The Sumerians, a sedentary people of Mesopotamia, were not far behind the Chinese. Their artwork depicts

Ill. I-1. Edwin Freeman driving the road horse Miss Dean Key to a road wagon. (Photographer/Sargent)

carts as early as 3000 B.C., although these were pulled by oxen or by onagers, descendants of the wild ass. It wasn't until 2600 B.C. that the pictorial art of the Sumerians, in the form of a royal seal, portrayed their king driving a pair of horses to a four-wheeled vehicle.

The benefits of the horse-drawn vehicle as a war machine and as an aid to farming quickly became evident. These uses gave impetus to the invention of more sophisticated driving equipment. The Sumerians developed an armored car which was drawn by four or five horses. By 2000 B.C. they were producing these war cars in numbers for use by the armies of rival leaders in their internecine wars.

In contrast to the nonexpansionist Sumerians, the Hittites and Mitann, nomadic tribesmen of the steppes, were continually bent upon expanding their territory. They instantly recognized the value of the Sumerian war car as a means to further their aims. As a result, these people were ultimately responsible for introducing horses and driving to a major part of the then populated world. However, they modified the heavy armored car of the Sumerians and developed a light, speedy, two-wheeled cart—the war chariot. It proved a valuable weapon, and masterful horsemanship during battle became a mark of distinction for warriors. In keeping with this emphasis, these people produced one of the earliest known volumes on horse training, a chariot-training manual called *The Training of the Horse.* It was written prior to 1000 B.C., in a language resembling Sanskrit, by Kikkuli, a Mitanni.

The Hittites took driving to Egypt, where horse-drawn transport replaced the litter as a fashionable mode of travel around 1500 B.C. At the battle of Kadesh the soldiers of Ramses II were routed by a contingent of Hittite chariots, but the pharaoh was saved from death by his harness horses. In gratitude, he announced to his army that he would feed them "with his own hands" upon return to his palace.

The war cart or chariot was introduced into Greece and eventually Rome (via Anatolia and/or Crete) around the middle of the second millennium (750–500 B.C.). Its use was relatively brief. By the fourth century, introduction of new military strategy employing cavalry put an end to its success as a war machine, although military leaders continued to use the chariot as transport. They could see the field of battle better than from horseback and their soldiers had a better view of them. Long after its demise as a weapon, the chariot became widely accepted as a racing vehicle. Greek history indicates that chariot races became part of the Olympic games in 680 B.C. Races for saddle horses were not introduced to the games until 564 B.C.

The harness horse was an integral part of civilized existence for several thousand years, and its usefulness increased and diversified together with human populations. For many centuries driving was a tool of farmers and soldiers and a luxury of the aristocracy. However, during the Middle Ages two changes occurred which greatly expanded the usefulness of the harness horse. The first of these changes was the development of uniform systems of roads. The Chinese well understood the importance of roads. During feudal times, each state adapted its roads to a particular axle gauge so that outsiders would be unable to drive on them. In an era of peaceful rule during the third century, an edict was published standardizing axles to facilitate communication and transport and thus draw the people of China together. In Europe, by the late Middle Ages, a system of roads existed that allowed harness horses to draw carts loaded with goods throughout the continent. The increase in trade and financial activity sparked by this relatively speedy and efficient way of moving products is considered to have played a major role in the rise of the Renaissance. A second change, the development of springs, made vehicular travel more appealing to civilians. Originally the body of a vehicle was attached directly to the undercarriage. Travel was rough and uncomfortable for the passengers. A primitive step toward springing is apparent in a cart that was found at a ninth-century Viking site in Oseberg, Norway. Its body is suspended above axles on concave supports. Later, the Hungarians experimented with a method of hanging the body of the vehicle by chains or leather straps from curved wooden staves that projected from the axles. The forerunner of modern springs seems to have appeared around the fourteenth century. These were curved, flexible metal supports placed between the undercarriage and the body of the vehicle. The harness also underwent some changes during the Middle Ages. Perhaps most important, the neck collar was perfected, replacing the primitive neck strap that interfered with breathing and ignored the principles of draft.

The utility of the harness horse reached its pinnacle between the seventeenth and the nineteenth centuries. During the 1600s the "European carriage" made its appearance. Smaller front wheels increased mobility, improved springs added comfort, a forward-slanting hood or enclosed cab kept passengers dry and warm, and better harnessing techniques allowed efficient multiple hitches to haul heavier loads faster over longer distances. Thereafter an increasingly complex society generated a need for all kinds of vehicles, ranging from carts, to coaches, to large commercial equipages. Carriage builders continually improved the functionality of the equipment, and standard shapes and styles of vehicles began to be produced. Ornamentation became important. Vehicles reflected the fashions of the times as well as the tastes of the owners.

The harness horse was necessary to civilized existence. He transported mail, supplies, and passengers. He pulled farm wagons, ambulances, fire wagons, and cannon. And he was raced for recreation. The uses of the harness horse and the variety of driving equipment increased and diversified until, as the United States 1900 census attests, there was one horse for every four people in the country. But the turn of the century also marked the beginning of decline. Acceptance of the internal-combustion engine erased in a few years an interrelationship and dependence of centuries. Victim of a whirlwind rush toward industrialization, the centuries-old bond between mankind and the horse appeared to be broken. Numbers of horses began to decrease worldwide and this trend continued until the 1960s when, for the first time in decades, equine population began to increase. Yes, horses were obsolete as beasts of burden, but humans, unable to break the bond, choose to make them coveted companions of increasing leisure time. Saddle sports led the resurgence, then the international equestrian community slowly stirred with interest in driving.

Today, driving is experiencing a full-scale revival. This discipline is no longer the domain of a few diehard coachmen in England, a handful of American breed-ring trainers, Eastern European dressage practitioners, royal traditionalists, and an assortment of nostalgia buffs. Horsemen, novice and experienced alike, are driving. The reasons are varied, but all agree that as horse sports become more competitive the unique benefits of driving are more obvious and desirable.

Driving, steeped as it is in centuries of practice, is proving to be a treasure chest. Farsighted horsemen and horsewomen are just beginning to explore the contents and to funnel their discoveries back into the mainstream of equestrian activity. One thing is clear: harness work can be an asset to any area of horsemanship. It can be a place to begin schooling, a training aid, a facet of conditioning, or a vacation for the horse. It is also an excellent area for older, overweight, out-of-condition, or handicapped, people who might not otherwise become involved or compete in a horse sport.

Driving the horse in harness is also an end in itself. The relatively young, intensely competitive sport of combined driving is just one example. Based on the three-day event, drivers perform a dressage test, negotiate a cross-country marathon, and drive an obstacle course. The excitement of this sport is reflected in its snowballing success; more events are planned and executed and more participants are competing locally, nationally, and internationally with each passing year.

But, perhaps most important, driving can be an unmatched private

Ill. I-2. Sallie Walrond driving Cottenham Loretto, an eight-year old Connemara gelding, to a skeleton gig. (Photographer/Terry Lubbuck)

pastime shared by a man or woman and a horse. Peel away pretty trappings—brass, patent leather, antique or competition vehicles, groom and spectators—and visualize a single horse drawing a light vehicle down a quiet track or along an empty country road. This is the essence of the sport. It is the development of gentle hands which communicate invisibly with an educated equine mouth. It is a horse free to balance without the weight of a rider. It is experiencing the cadence of the trot, the whirr of the wheels, the reflections beading along muscular hindquarters. It is also a low voice, a revolving ear, and an answering change of gait. This harmony between a single horse and driver silhouetted against the ancient colorful tapestry of history is the basis of driving today. The achievement of this harmony is the purpose of the following chapters.

The first three chapters are devoted to the elements of driving—horse, equipment, and elementary training. The fourth chapter prepares the driver to take the reins. The six remaining chapters take a look at specialized areas of driving, including the breed ring, antique carriage competition, and harness racing. The unique emphasis of each different field can be an aid to understanding and improved performance by individual drivers on their "home ground," be it a backyard pleasure drive or a combined driving event.

1

THE HORSE

Equestrian sport is divided into two major categories: driving and riding. Each category has numerous subdivisions. For instance, the harness horse can be a race horse, a show horse, or a pleasure horse. The same is true of the saddle horse. And within these three sections there is more segmentation. The show horse can excel as a roadster or an antique carriage horse. In fact, like colors within the spectrum, the variations become subtler and more numerous with closer scrutiny. In the end, each individual horse is a specialist. He is trained to develop or schooled to polish skills deemed necessary by his handlers to perform a very specific task.

Obviously, a horse is not born a "specialist." Natural ability plus days,

Ill. 1-1. Gayle Warren driving Arabian National Formal Driving Champion Stallion, Mon-Bo.

months, even years of training are necessary to develop the specialized horse. The purpose of the following chapters is to present a body of information that can aid readers in recognizing and advancing the equine talents that are special to driving horses. Specifically, the text will discuss understanding, appraising, equipping, training, showing, and enjoying harness horses. But before we delve into the subtleties that set driving horses apart from other horses, we should examine some important similarities.

Common Bonds

Horses of the various domestic breeds are more alike than different from one another. They share a common chromosome count, which sets them apart as a distinct species from other mammals and gives them certain physical characteristics in common. They all have a similar structure, making them capable of a predictable range of movement, and they are all subject to the same instinctive urges.

A basic knowledge of equine structure, movement, perception, and temperament is helpful at every level of horsemanship. Much time is spent schooling horses in an attempt to train them to perform at the peak of their capabilities on command. It is time and energy wasted if we work against nature's design. An understanding of the mental and physical framework of the average horse—of its limitations, including a powerful instinct to run from danger and an inflexible spine that limits lateral movement, as well as of its potentials—is essential to success as a horseman or horsewoman.

A familiarity with the skeletal and muscular structure of the horse is the first requisite. Detailed anatomical charts are outside the scope of this book. If you would like to obtain this information, I recommend a text such as *Anatomy of Domestic Animals* by Sisson and Grossman. The points of the horse, the external anatomical characteristics, are shown here (Ill. 1-2). The names of the various parts of the horse are the foundation of an age-old equestrian language. This terminology will be used throughout the following pages.

Anatomical structure determines balance, and it is loss of balance that initiates action. The laws of physics inextricably bind the three (structure, balance, movement) together. A horse standing relaxed and motionless is an example of *static balance.* In this position, with head and neck extended, 60 percent of the animal's weight is in front of an imaginary center line. This is the clue to understanding the mechanics of the horse in motion. The head and neck, a mobile pendulum, are capable of changing structural shape, initiating moments of balance and imbalance as weight is shifted and the horse begins to move. A horse in motion alternates between moments of instability and firmness of position. This is *dynamic balance.*

Gait is the term used to describe types of equine movement. The majority of horses naturally execute a walk, trot, canter, and gallop. Selective breeding

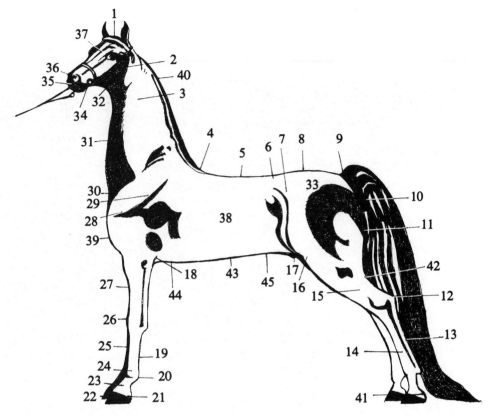

Ill. 1-2.   The points of the horse:

1. Poll
2. Cheek
3. Neck
4. Withers
5. Back
6. Loins
7. Point of hip
8. Croup
9. Dock
10. Point of buttock
11. Buttock
12. Hock
13. Flexor tendon
14. Hind cannon
15. Gaskin
16. Stifle
17. Sheath
18. Elbow
19. Tendons
20. Ergot
21. Coronet
22. Hoof
23. Pastern
24. Fetlock
25. Fore cannon
26. Knee
27. Forearm
28. Point of shoulder
29. Shoulder
30. Jugular groove
31. Windpipe
32. Jowl
33. Hindquarters
34. Chin groove
35. Muzzle
36. Nostril
37. Forehead
38. Barrel
39. Chest
40. Crest
41. Bulb of heel
42. Hamstring
43. Underline
44. Girth
45. Belly

has led to other ways of moving, such as the running walk of the Tennessee Walker or the pace exhibited by some families of American Standardbreds. Training accounts for important "learned" movements, for example, the rein-back and the sidepass. A brief description of the workings of common gaits follows. More specialized information about gaits is included in later chapters.

The *walk* is characterized by a longitudinal shift of weight. An up-and-down movement of the head and neck initiates the weight shift and acts as a balancing gesture. The walk is described as a lateral gait because the legs on one side of the body support the horse while the legs on the opposite side move forward. It is a four-beat gait, meaning that each hoof touches the ground individually in a predictable sequence. Observe a horse walking and begin counting as the right hind leg moves forward: the right hind will touch down as beat number one; number two will be the right front; the third beat is the left hind; and the fourth beat is the left front. The average horse walks at a speed of 4 to 6 miles per hour.

In the *trot* weight is displaced from side to side. A horse is well balanced at the trot; it is not necessary for him to move his head and neck to maintain stability to the degree he must at other gaits. The reason for this is that the trot is a diagonal movement. At all times the horse has two feet—one on each side of his body—on the ground. The cadence of the trot is two beats. Diagonal front and hind legs touch the ground simultaneously. For example, the right hind and the left front touch down as one beat; the left hind and right front establish the second beat. The speed of the average trot is 8 miles per hour.

The *canter*, like the walk, is recognized by a front to rearward displacement of weight, resulting in an extreme up-and-down movement of the head

Ill. 1-3. Movement.

and neck to maintain balance. It is a three-beat gait, less stable than the walk or trot, because at moments the horse must balance with only one hoof on the ground. Although much emphasis is placed on the leading leg, it is generally acknowledged that the diagonal hind leg moves forward first. A typical canter sequence on a circle tracking left would be: beat one—the right hind; beat two—the left hind and right front in unison; beat three—the left front or leading leg. The speed of the average canter is 10 to 12 miles per hour.

The *gallop* is a distinct gait. It is not vital to harness work. Only rarely is a harness horse asked to gallop, but drivers agree that an understanding of its characteristics is helpful when a young or spirited horse decides to forgo dependence on human handlers and respond to the flight instinct. The gallop is like the canter in regard to weight-shift and balance, but because of the faster forward movement it becomes a four-beat gait. The hooves that touch down in unison at the canter, strike individually at the gallop, creating a rapid four-beat gait. Gallop beats occur as follows: beat one—right hind; beat two— left hind; beat three—right front; beat four—left front (leading leg). In the average gallop the horse moves at 16 to 18 miles per hour.

How a horse moves is important to understand, and equally important is *why* a horse moves. Every horse is subject to instinctive drives that are related to survival and procreation of the species. Although tempered by domestication and modified by training, it is these drives that determine the behavior of every horse. An awareness of these basic urges will aid us in overriding some and satisfying others.

The flight instinct is probably the strongest natural impulse to which the equine mind responds. Horses have survived through the eons because they are fleet and surefooted and run from danger. Of course, their perception of danger and ours is often dissimilar and this can get the unwary horseperson into trouble. We will examine this point in more detail below when we look at the equine senses.

A second strong instinct is the herd instinct. Horses are by nature social animals and are more confident in a group. This proclivity can be an aid or a detriment to training, depending on the situation.

Horses also establish pecking orders. One horse is boss and each additional animal takes an assigned place in the ranks. This behavioral trait is of particular interest to drivers who use horses in groups.

All horses need food and water. This very basic urge will be discussed in the section "Daily and Routine Care," p. 13. But another, sometimes overlooked, equally basic companion need is daily movement. Movement is important as much for the physical well-being of the horse as for its mental health. A great many stable vices can be prevented by satisfying this instinctive drive. Prior to domestication, horses wandered to find sufficient forage to survive. The stall-bound horse, however, finds food and water closeby. Hunger and thirst are satisfied, but the natural impulse to wander is not. Often, out of frustration, these animals develop behavioral abnormalities—weaving, cribbing, wood-chewing, and the like. Some horses are more subject to the need for movement than others. One theory suggests that those animals whose ancestors lived in areas of sparse vegetation and traveled farther for a day's food, generally horses of desert ancestry, are more susceptible than are "cold-blooded" horses, whose ancestors found forage easily.

How horses perceive their environment is another common bond which holds many clues to their behavior. The species is equipped with a unique set of senses, acute in some ways and inaccurate in others. This disparity has puzzled and disconcerted horseowners since the beginning of mankind's association with the horse.

To begin with, horses have an acute sense of hearing. Large, mobile ears act as an early-warning system cuing the possibility of danger, be it a predator in the brush or a note of hysteria in a handler's voice.

Their sense of smell is keen. Smell is another defense against predators and a means of determining the palatability of food and water. It is also used as a medium for recognition. For example, horses blow in each others' nostrils as a greeting.

A discerning sense of taste is characteristic. Horses are able to sift through feed and remove foreign objects. A horse will sometimes refuse to drink water from an unfamiliar source. A copper or iron mouthpiece can soothe a restive or tense horse that is uncomfortable with a nickel or stainless-steel bit.

Horses are sensitive to touch. They are known to communicate via "grooming"—scratching and chewing a partner with lips and teeth. It is commonly believed that daily brushing of the coat is essential to the well-being of a stabled horse and can be therapeutic.

Vision in horses is poor and inaccurate. They are color blind and have irregular retinas contributing to inefficient focusing. Placement of the eyes on the sides of the head provides bilateral rear vision but also probably causes double frontal views. This would explain why horses shy at dark spots on the ground, blowing scraps of paper, and puddles. To a horse, these objects may appear blurry and double focused.

Finally, before we delve into the specifics of harness horses, there is one last common bond worthy of a closer look: equine temperament. Temperament is the product of the preceding factors modified by individual environment. On the surface the horse is a large, warm-blooded quadruped, a vegetarian who survives by running from danger. However, a closer look reveals the horse to be also a gentle, trusting, and sensitive animal. A horse will allow a handler's command to override his most basic instincts or respond with great heart in spite of fatigue or pain. The equine temperament places horsemen and horsewomen in a position of cherished though awesome responsibility.

Attributes of a Driving Horse

The harness horse is singular in the world of horse sport. The most obvious difference is that he does not carry a person upon his back. Instead, he is asked to pull his handler in a wheeled vehicle (or push against a collar

Ill. 1-4.   Peter Morin driving a pair of Morgan mares (Greene Acres Debbie and Otter Brook Alida) belonging to Otterbrook Farm.

of some sort and thus draw a vehicle—this is a matter of semantics). He takes his direction from a disembodied voice some distance behind. The driver's physical presence is transmitted by his handling of the reins and whip. The horse, more often than not, can't see the driver because of the common practice of fitting a harness horse with blinders which obscure the animal's rear, and in some cases peripheral, vision. A driving horse is freer to find his own balance because he does not have to compensate for the weight of a rider, but he is encumbered by the length, breadth, and weight of the driving equipment. Taking this information into consideration, it is easy to imagine the special qualities an ideal harness horse might possess: a blend of temperament, conformation, and training.

The ideal harness horse is a rarity. Each dedicated harness enthusiast with a bit of luck is said to have one such horse in a lifetime. And, to complicate matters more, the definition of *ideal* varies from area to area within the sport. Fortunately, every horse of reasonably sound mind and body, given sensible training, can be expected to be a "good" driving horse. Furthermore, every horse will possess a number of the attributes of the ideal horse.

Disposition is the primary concern. The old adage "beauty is only skin deep" applies with a vengeance to horses. A nervous, shy, sour, spoiled, or vicious horse—however handsome he may be—hinders enjoyment and introduces fear, even danger, to the sport. Unfortunately these horses are often

the end result of cruel or thoughtless handling, though some have a biochemical basis for their disturbance. I firmly believe a sound mind is as much a
prerequisite for a successful harness horse as is a sound body. And horse psy-
chiatry is part of the skill of a talented trainer.

Conformation is a vital secondary concern. Not only does conformation affect athletic ability, but it also to a great extent determines soundness.
A description of good working conformation follows. Only a licensed veterinarian (after a thorough examination) is qualified to determine if a horse is
sound.

The head of the average horse of good conformation should feature a
broad, flat forehead with plenty of breadth ("brain space") between the eyes.
A large, softly expressive eye is desirable. Many horseman insist they can
determine the worth of a horse by looking at the eye. Avoid lumps or bumps
between the eyes or on the nose as well as misshapen eyes. These can cause
distortion or be an indication of impairments of vision.

A harness horse is expected to have a higher head carriage than a saddle

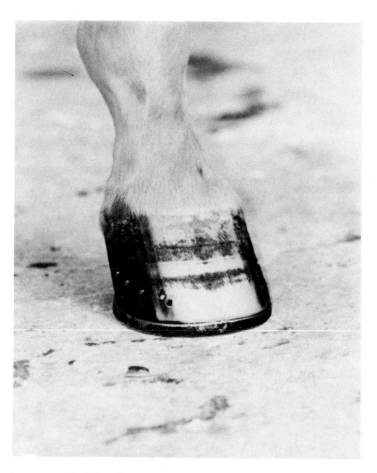

Ill. 1-5. A symmetrical hoof.

horse. A long, well-formed neck with a natural curve from breast to jowl is desirable. The throttle should be refined. A coarse throttle interferes with the flexion necessary for many aspects of driving. Also avoid overly cresty or ewe-necked animals.

The shoulder is of great importance. It should be sloping rather than upright. An ideal shoulder is "laid back" toward the heart girth (see angle between 28 and 4 in Ill. 1-2). A good shoulder permits a horse to move with knee-popping high action when collected and with toe-pointing extensions. Training can never overcome the disadvantages of a straight shoulder.

A deep body is an asset to the harness horse. A greater-than-average width from withers to underline coupled with well-sprung ribs permits maximum lung expansion and promotes stamina. A strong back is neither long nor swayed, so a close-coupled body is desirable. The chest should be reasonably deep and wide. A broad chest is excellent for great strength in short bursts. A deep, well-muscled chest is better for the long haul. The underline should be taut. Avoid a droopy underline, which is indicative of weak abdominal muscles.

Entire volumes have been published about equine legs. It is an art to be able to evaluate or predict the future soundness and service of a horse's legs. There is an old saying among horsemen: "It isn't straight legs so much as straight-going legs." This is good advice. Inspect legs closely while a horse is standing, but reserve judgment until after you have watched him move.

Briefly, a good foreleg features a straight, well-muscled forearm, a large flat knee, and a clean cannon bone. The presence of nicks, lumps, or abrasions on or below the cannon suggest the horse interferes or overreaches. Splints (bumps on the cannon bone, the result of calcification) are serious if they are close to the knee or beneath the flexor tendons. Tendons should be tight and flat. Avoid short, steep pasterns as well as those with excessive slope. Toeing in, toeing out, knock-knees, or knees that deviate laterally may also be signs of problems.

A good hind leg shares many characteristics with a good foreleg. A muscular, smooth gaskin, a clean cannon, tight tendons, and a moderately sloping pastern are prerequisites. Viewed from behind, the hocks and cannons of good hind legs should be parallel.

The hoof is a delicate and complicated structure. Its healthy functioning is so important to the value of the whole horse that the saying "no hoof, no hoss" is not to be taken lightly. A sound hoof is symmetrical and unblemished. The coronet band should be faultless, without visible scarring or bulging. The frog should be firm and odor-free, the sole cupped, and the heels open. More detailed information about hoof function and care can be found in the section of this chapter titled, "Daily and Routine Care," p. 13.

In summary, the attributes of the harness horse include conformation, temperament, and training. Good working conformation is essential, though the ideal harness horse should also be upheaded, a stylish mover, and generally of more substance than the ideal saddle horse. As to temperament, he must be sensible without being dull. A horse with a bright, willing attitude who moves freely forward on command is ideal. Conformation is genetic. Temperament is the result of genetics and environment. Training is the province of horsemen and horsewomen. Chapter 3, therefore, covers basic training, and succeeding chapters explore elements of training necessary to more specialized realms of driving.

The Talent Pool

As I have said, any horse or pony, barring serious physical or mental defects, can learn to be driven. It is worth noting, however, that generations of selective breeding have produced types of horses particuarly suited to driving. Some breeds have been used as harness horses for centuries, but as driving becomes more popular and diversified, breeds not customarily considered driving horses are entering the field. An example of a traditional breed is the Hackney Horse revered by English coachmen. For many years the elegant carriage and classic action of these animals in harness has been unrivaled. On the other hand, a relative newcomer, the American Quarter Horse, is excelling in harness for vastly different reasons. Sense, stamina, and agility make the Quarter Horse an exceptional combined-driving candidate.

Ill. 1-6.   The Hackney Horse.

Ill. 1-7. Ann Knoll driving Knollcrest Superjet, a Morgan pleasure horse. (Photographer/Equus Studios)

Ill. 1-8. An American Quarter Horse.

Ill. 1-9.   Liz Turner driving Torch Club, an American Standardbred, at a combined-driving event.

The talent pool is large but the choice between breeds is less difficult than it first appears. Appropriateness is the key word. Some horses are appropriate for certain drivers or types of vehicle or specialties within the sport. For instance, an Appaloosa and a phaeton do not belong together. An Arabian is not competitive in a harness race, nor is a timid driver comfortable with a high-strung horse. Tradition, suitability and, perhaps most important, personal goals must be your guidelines.

A recognized breed makes an excellent choice for a driving horse. Breed standards encourage magnification of uniform, beneficial characteristics. This is particularly useful when looking for a pair or a group of matched animals. However, crossbred and grade horses with admirable qualities abound.

A list of old and new breeds specially qualified for driving follows. An appendix at the end of the text contains addresses of some popular breed registries. Most registries will, upon request, send detailed information about the unique attributes of their breed. Also, although this book deals primarily with light driving horses, some heavy horse and pony breeds customarily used in harness are listed as well.

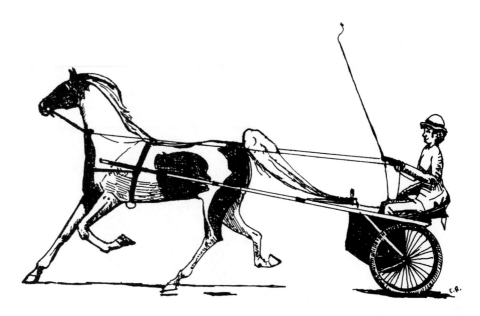

Ill. 1-10. A pinto American Saddlebred pleasure-driving horse.

Light Horses	Heavy Horses	Ponies
Andalusian	Belgian	Connemara
Appaloosa	Clydesdale	Exmoor
Arabian	Percheron	Fell
Cleveland Bay	Shire	Hackney
Friesian	Suffolk	Haflinger
Gelderlander		Icelandic
Hackney		Norwegian Fjord
Hanovarian		Pony of Americas
Holsteiner		Shetland
Lipizzaner		Welsh
Morgan		
Oldenburg		
Quarter Horse		
Saddlebred		
Standardbred		
Trakehner		

Daily and Routine Care

As the realm of harness sport becomes increasingly sophisticated, there is less and less room for the carriage enthusiast who keeps his antique vehicle in a climatically controlled house while his horse forages, unsheltered, in an

Ill. 1-11. The harder a horse works, the harder we, in turn, must work to maintain his physical and mental health. Anita Mellot driving Fancy, a Morab owned by the California Carriage and Harness Company.

unkept pasture. The most beautiful vehicle loses its appeal when drawn by a rough-coated, undernourished horse whose feet have not been trimmed for months. The horse is no longer self-sufficient. He is dependent upon his domesticators for the most basic necessities of life. The harder a horse is expected to work for his handlers, the harder they, in turn, must work to maintain his physical and mental health. It is a painstaking and time-consuming responsibility. Luckily, it is also a labor of love.

First, every horse has a basic nutritional need. Nutrition is the process whereby food is metabolized and absorbed into the body to be used to fuel all equine functions. All horses are individuals. Each horse requires different amounts of the same nutrients.

Water is the most vital nutrient. A horse will lose condition faster and more critically from lack of water than from lack of any other nutrient. Three-fifths of the body weight of the average horse is water. Yet the water level is not stable. Water leaves the body in the form of sweat and urine. This water must be replaced. A horse drinks between 5 and 15 gallons of water a day, depending upon variables such as size, activity, and feed. Free access to water at all times (with the notable exception of an overheated horse) is indispensable to a program of sound daily care.

Carbohydrates and proteins, the nutrients that provide energy for body functions, are the next concern. Good-quality hay (leafy, fine, green, dust-

and mold-free) and grain (clean, fresh, dust-free) contain these nutrients in a form the equine digestive tract can utilize. The standard 1,000-pound horse requires 22 to 30 pounds of feed per day. The ratio of hay to grain depends upon a number of factors. First and foremost is the nutritive value of the hay. Grain is an excellent supplement to increase energy intake. However, a mature horse who is not working can thrive on good hay alone. Young, lactating, or hard-working horses require the extra protein commonly found in cereal grains. As a rule of thumb, a horse that is losing weight is not receiving enough energy and an overweight horse is receiving too much.

Legume hay (alfalfa) or grass hay (timothy) of the same quality are equally suitable, although less alfalfa is required to produce an equivalent amount of energy. Corn, oats, and barley are the grains commonly fed to horses. Corn weighs twice as much as oats, with barley falling in between. Never measure feed by volume—one cup of corn contains twice the protein of one cup of oats. Greater weight of feed indicates a higher energy content.

Horses have a limited ability to digest fibrous material. Coarse, woody, stemmy hay and thick-hulled grains pass through the digestive tract unchanged. The horse is unable to crack the surface of these feeds and release the nutrients inside. Freshly crimped grain and leafy, fine-stemmed hay are solutions to this problem.

The digestive tract of the horse has a small capacity. Several small feedings per day are recommended. Also, any change in type, quality, or quantity of feed should be made gradually to avoid upsetting a delicate system.

Vitamins A, C, D, E, K, and the B-complex are also essential in varying amounts to the healthy horse. Many of these vitamins can be synthesized by the equine digestive tract from hay, grain, soil, even sunlight. What is available naturally changes from one locale to another. Supplements can be given, but too much is often as harmful as too little. Check with your veterinarian to determine the insufficiencies in your area before you supplement. If you purchase a supplement, be sure it is fresh. Time and heat rapidly destroy vitamin potency.

Salt is imperative to the normal body function of the horse. Free access to salt is the only adequate way to fill this need. A salt block or salt in granular form should be available in the pasture or stall.

Calcium and phosphorous also are important to the equine system. Correct proportion counts as much as availability, however. Serious skeletal disorders and an inability to achieve energy transfer can result from an imbalance of these minerals. A one-to-one ratio of calcium to phosphorous seems to be accepted as correct at the present time.

Horses require trace amounts of magnesium, iodine, copper, iron, selenium, zinc, fluoride, and sulfur and possibly manganese. A mineralized salt block or a free-choice mineral feeder should be provided.

The well-fed horse also needs shelter. Wind, rain, snow, heat, and flies are not just annoying facts of life to be endured by horses; they can be detrimental. A stall is customary housing, but a three-sided shed is sufficient for the pastured horse. The stall requires daily maintenance to keep it manure-free. The pasture should be dragged periodically to work the manure into the soil and should occasionally be reseeded. Manure should be disposed of some distance from the stable and a program of fly control religiously practiced.

Stall-bound horses or horses who do not enjoy the company of other horses benefit from daily grooming. Grooming is therapeutic as well as cosmetic. Horses are companionable animals and need to be touched and stroked to promote a sense of well-being. A rubber curry used in a circular motion stimulates the circulation (do not curry legs and face) and brings dust and dirt to the surface. A hard brush removes debris from the coat. A soft brush finishes the job by smoothing the surface. Hand rubbing and toweling are enjoyed by most horses; the effect is to bring oils to the surface of the hair, adding a natural glow to the coat.

The hooves of the horse require daily as well as periodic care. The hoof is a complicated structure with a delicate balance of component parts. These parts must work together to absorb the force of the weight of the whole horse

Ill. 1-12. Bob Carver, a professional farrier, at work cupping the sole.

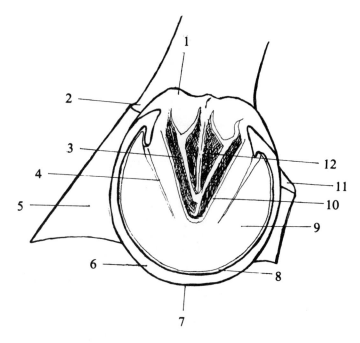

Ill. 1-13. Parts of the hoof:
1. *Bulb of heel*
2. *Coronet band*
3. *Frog*
4. *Bar*
5. *Hoof wall*
6. *Ground border of hoof wall*

7. *Toe*
8. *White line*
9. *Sole*
10. *Lateral groove*
11. *Heel*
12. *Central groove*

connecting with the ground as he moves. The frog stretches, the heels and bars expand, the hoof wall flexes and spreads. In this way the hooves act as shock absorbers and distribute the force of concussion. Only a professional can lay the groundwork for sound hoof performance. A competent farrier needs to trim, shoe, or reshoe a horse at regular six- to eight-week intervals to keep hooves accurately angled and balanced.

Each set of hooves is unique and requires individual care. However, good hooves all have certain factors in common. A good hoof is symmetrical, with a naturally smooth and lustrous surface. Cracks, bulges, ridges, or furrows are signs of trouble, as are dished or flared profiles. Generally, the sole is concave and longer than it is wide. As a rule of thumb, the angle of the hoof and the angle of the pastern are the same. A balanced hoof displays a steeper inside than outside wall. The heels should be open and their angle the same as the toe or slightly steeper.

Daily hoof care includes cleaning and dressing the hoof. Clean around the frog and inside the shoe to remove hard objects that could cause bruises and manure that could cause the fungus disease called thrush. To remain flexible, the hoof has to maintain a level of moisture. Dry hooves should be moistened with water and then the hoof wall and sole coated with a dressing to

Ill. 1-14. Daily exercise is an important element of everyday care. Susan Carter driving Miraj, a part-Arab gelding.

seal in the moisture. Climate and locale determine how often this is necessary, but once to three times a week is usual.

Exercise is also necessary for the stabled horse. Exercise improves circulation, promotes digestion, establishes and maintains muscle tone, and eases boredom. A workout is excellent, but free time in a pasture or paddock is a good alternative. A walk on a lead shank is far better than no time at all outside the stall. A walk to a grassy patch and few minutes grazing on the end of a shank is a treat for any stall-bound horse.

Certain periodic routine care is essential for optimum equine health. A veterinarian can supply specific information. Basically, every horse must be wormed at regular (six-week to three-month) intervals. When uncontrolled, internal parasites cause scarring of the walls of the digestive tract. This is irreversible and eventually fatal. The only solution is regular worming. A number of annual innoculations are also recommended. An initial series and regular boosters for tetanus, eastern and western encephalomyelitis, influenza, and rhinopneumonitis are necessary for most horses. Dental care is also necessary. The teeth should be checked regularly and filed (floated) to remove sharp points which could prevent efficient grinding of feed and thereby interfere with utilization of nutrients.

Armed with this basic information about the horse, we are ready to leave the stable and explore another facet of driving. On to the harness room for a look at driving equipment.

2
BASIC EQUIPMENT

There is more than tangible pleasure to be had from the equipment of driving. There is also the glamour of nostalgia. A little imagination conjures up a well-stocked harness room and carriage house. Beveled-glass carriage lanterns bathe the scene in a warm glow. The glitter of polished brass, stainless steel, and chrome, the gleam of sleek patent leather, and the poignant odor of supple, substantial harness leather gratify the eyes and nostrils. The gentle light reflects off shafts, poles, and harmonious wheels of hickory, ash, oak, and perhaps lemon wood. Lustrous, classic colors—natural wood, coach green, burgundy, black—weave together in a rich tapestry. The wood of the vehicles is subtly, impeccably pin-striped or lined and, in some cases, formally adorned with small, tasteful monograms. Holly whips, plush

Ill. 2-1. Postillion carriage drawn by black Friesian Horses which brought the Royal Family of the Netherlands to the opening ceremonies of the World Driving Championships at Apeldoorn, Holland in 1982. (Photograph/Courtesy of Driving Digest Magazine)

upholstery, and lap robes add a sumptuous touch, and the specter of a gloved, liveried coachman completes the scene. These are the wonderful accouterments of formal driving as it existed a century ago and does, to a large extent, today.

Driving equipment was the first gear invented for the horse. In the beginning, several thousand years B.C., it was primitive and inefficient. A harness consisted of strips of rawhide wrapped around the neck of the horse and tied to two poles. The poles dragged on the ground behind the horse and a hammock of leather joined the poles to provide load space. The load potential and range of vehicles improved dramatically with the development of the wheel approximately 5,000 years ago. Crude, solid wooden wheels eventually gave way to lighter cut-out or spoked wheels rimmed with metal. The neck yoke was in use by 2,000 B.C. Although it had drawbacks—the yoke strap pressed against the jugular vein and windpipe of the horse and a high point of traction severely limited capacity—this innovation is considered the origin of modern harness. In fact, neck yokes are still used in parts of the world today. Breast- and neck-collar harness first appeared in Asia. They were in general use in Europe by A.D. 800. The singletree appeared a few centuries later. Both the collars and the singletree (also whiffletree or swingletree—a mobile bar to which the traces are attached) improved efficiency by lowering the point of traction, freeing the shoulders of the horse, and equalizing the load on the traces. Improvements have continued as the history of driving lengthens.

Basic Harness

The primary function of harness is to attach a horse to a vehicle. Additionally, to ensure optimum performance from the horse, the harness must be comfortable. A third factor, the safety of the harness, determines the well-being of the vehicle and its contents. These three qualities have guided the development of harness for centuries. For this reason, the elementary parts of the harness are conventional. Esthetics may determine cut, color, and ornamentation; but efficiency, comfort, and safety dictate the design of bridle, bit, reins, collar, traces, pad or saddle, crupper, and wraps or breeching.

A harness bridle and a riding bridle have basic similarities. Both consist of a crownpiece, browband, throttle strap, noseband or cavesson, and cheekpieces. The browband slides over the crownpiece and is positioned across the forehead just below, but never against, the base of the ears. Harness browbands are often ornamental, decorated with brass or colorful patent leather. The throat lash buckles to the right side of the crownpiece and extends under the jaw of the horse ending in a buckle on the left crownpiece. Generally, the throat lash or strap is adjusted a hole tighter than a riding bridle to prevent the horse from hooking the bridle on a shaft and pulling it off. However, the strap should never be so tight that it interferes with normal breathing. The upper end of the cheekpiece on either side buckles to the crown-

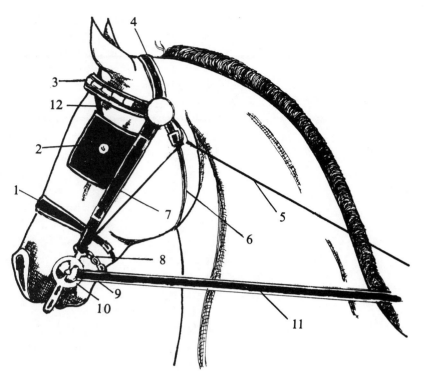

Ill. 2-2. The Driving Bridle:
1. *Noseband*
2. *Blinder*
3. *Browband*
4. *Crownpiece*
5. *Sidecheck*
6. *Throttle strap*
7. *Cheekpiece*
8. *Curb chain*
9. *Billet of rein*
10. *Liverpool bit*
11. *Rein*
12. *Blinder stay*

Ill. 2-2A. Cavesson.

piece. A noseband slides through leather keepers on the cheekpieces. A noseband is correctly positioned two large fingers' width below the cheekbones. The noseband buckles below the jaw and is properly tensioned when it admits two fingers. Its primary function is to prevent the blinders from being pulled away from the eyes of the horse when rein pressure on the bit causes the cheekpieces to gap. A cavesson should be used if it is necessary to hold the mouth closed. A cavesson encircles the nose, but does not pass through the cheekpieces of the bridle. It has its own leather hanger and is independent of the headstall (the bridle without bit and reins attached), though this (the hanger strap) can be threaded through the loops of the browband to unite the bridle. A cavesson can be worn lower and tighter than a noseband, but use discretion. A cavesson that is too low traps a fold of skin between the bit and the leather. Bit action pinches the skin and eventually rubs it sore. The cheekpieces buckle around the bit.

Two additional bridle parts not common to riding bridles are proving to be the most controversial elements of harness. Blinders (winkers or blinkers) and bearing reins are standard to most harness bridles. Blinders are pieces of leather that can be rectangular, round, square, or in the shape of a shell, D, or hatchet. They are attached to the cheekpieces below the browband and above the noseband. The outer covering is often patent leather decorated with a tiny crest or monogram; the insides are lined with soft, smooth leather. Stays—flexible, tubular leather straps—buckle to the crownpiece and are stitched to the upper inside edge of the blinders. The function of blinders is to cover the eyes and eliminate rear vision. They must be carefully fitted with one-third of the blinder above the eye of the horse, and the stays adjusted to keep the blinder from touching the eye. Controversy has arisen over the need for blinders, particularly among combined driving and dressage enthusiasts, who expect their horses to perform difficult maneuvers and negotiate obstacles and who object to restricting the animals' field of vision. Basically, blinders are a justifiable safety feature. They prevent a horse from taking fright and bolting, which can happen in reaction to sunlight reflecting off wheels, a passenger who makes a sudden movement, or a driver who appears to make a threatening gesture with the whip. Traditional blinders inhibit peripheral as well as rear vision. However, a new type of blinder is gaining rapid acceptance and may be the solution to the controversy. The modern blinder is cupped, obscuring only rear vision and permitting full peripheral vision. Some horses are more frightened by the noise than the sight of a disturbance; others are so dependent that they lose confidence if they cannot see their handlers. These "rare" horses should be started in harness without blinders; eventually the aid can be introduced.

It is interesting to note in regard to blinders, that American Standardbred trotters traditionally race without them, and that British military horses are trained to drive without them, as are many commercial horses. A bridle without blinders is an "open" bridle; one with blinders is termed a "closed" bridle.

Bearing reins, also called checkreins, are another unique harness bridle feature. Initially, a leather strap buckled to a separate "check" bit, passed through keepers on the cheekpieces and rings suspended from the crownpiece, and attached to a hook (Mckinney hook) on the saddle or pad. This type of bearing rein is called a sidecheck. A second type of check, the overcheck or Kemble Jackson check, was designed for a racing trotter in 1853. It also buckles to a separate "check" bit, but the leather strap passes up the center of the face, between the ears, through slots on the crownpiece, and attaches to the Mckinney hook. The sidecheck was devised to prevent a horse from dropping its head (as it might do to swipe at a fly or grab a mouthful of grass) and inadvertently hooking the bridle or reins over a shaft and pulling the bridle off in the ensuing struggle. On the other hand, the overcheck was designed as an aid for the racing trainer; by holding the head of the horse up and the nose out, ideal racing form is easier to achieve. Soon after fast trotters came into vogue in America, most American-made harness sported overchecks. This is still true today, though a gradual change is occurring as drivers realize the suitability of sidechecks for some styles of driving. An exception is the breed-ring show horse, which is traditionally shown with a half-cheek snaffle, an overcheck, and a martingale in order to quickly achieve an upheaded, high-moving way of going. The use of this equipment will be discussed in chapter 6.

A bearing rein is a safety device and a training aid. When properly adjusted, it comes into play if the horse drops its head too low. However, there is some disagreement among trainers over how low is "too low." Breed-ring trainers agree a checkrein is too short if a horse cannot flex at the poll. Other drivers insist the checkrein should be loose when the horse is standing relaxed. Needless to say, there is hearty contention between the two schools of thought.

There are several types of bits customarily used by trainers and drivers of harness horses. Some of these also serve as riding bits. A few are specialized driving bits. Information on bitting the young or green harness horse is included in chapter 3. A discussion of bit action and its relation to driving and the driver appears in chapter 4. More information about bits considered correct for various styles of driving is contained in chapters 6 through 10. The half-cheek snaffle, the double ring or Wilson snaffle, and the liverpool curb bit are the most common bits specifically designed for driving.

Driving reins (occasionally termed "lines") must be strong, substantial, and supple. Driving reins used with coachman-driven and pleasure-driving carriages are generally brown throughout, although less expensive and commercial harness are supplied with black or part-black reins. Reins should fit the hands of the driver. A rein width of 1 inch (or slightly more) is suitable for large, long-fingered hands. Seven-eights or three-quarters of an inch is comfortable for small hands or short fingers. The ends of the reins held by the driver are joined by stitching, a buckle, or a buckle and swivel snap. Some drivers prefer to bypass the buckle and hold the reins together with the keeper. This method of joining is less permanent and permits the reins to pull apart in case the driver becomes tangled in an accident. A type of rein designed for horses trained to be "up in the bridle" (race horses, park horses, road-

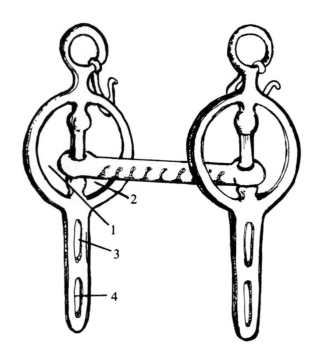

Ill. 2-3.   Liverpool bit:
1. *Rough cheek*   3. *Middle bar*
2. *Plain cheek*   4. *Bottom bar*

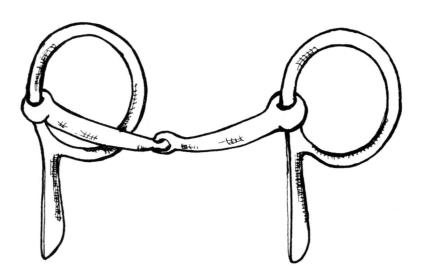

Ill. 2-4.   Half-cheek snaffle.

sters) has leather loops or handholds to increase driver security. Reins are threaded through terrets on the collar and the saddle or pad. The billet end of the rein is buckled around the bit. Correct length of rein is an important

Ill. 2-5. Single driving harness featuring breast collar, overcheck, and wrap straps instead of breeching.

consideration and varies from horse to horse and vehicle to vehicle. Reins should not be so short that the driver has to sit on the edge of his or her seat to reach their juncture, nor so long they can wrap around the legs of the driver or passengers. The section of the reins handled by the driver is always brown to prevent harness black (a dressing used on the black parts of the harness) from rubbing off on clothing.

The harness collar and its trace attachments make it possible for the horse to pull the vehicle. The force exerted by the horse as it moves forward into the collar causes the traces to become taut. If the horse continues to move forward, the vehicle moves. The act of drawing or pulling is "draft." A horse is said to be "in draft" when it is up in the collar and the traces are taut. The segment of the harness at which draft (drawing or pulling) is initiated is the "point of traction."

Collars are of two types: neck and breast collars. Neck collars ring the neck and rest against the shoulders of the horse. They are heavily padded and leather-covered. Neck collars are made to fit an individual horse exactly. They are not adjustable and therefore not interchangeable from horse to horse. Hames, twin metal arms, fit into grooves surrounding the collar and are linked and strapped securely together. Traces attach to the draft eye of the hames. Neck collars are more comfortable for horses pulling heavy loads

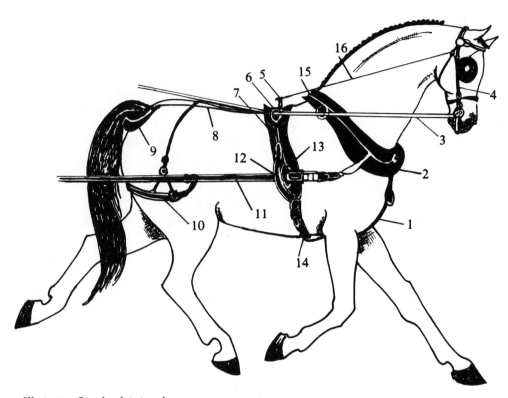

Ill. 2-6. Single driving harness:

1. *False martingale*
2. *Neck collar*
3. *Rein*
4. *Driving bridle*
5. *Bearing-rein hook*
6. *Rein terret*
7. *Saddle*
8. *Crupper strap*
9. *Crupper (dockpiece)*
10. *Breeching*
11. *Trace*
12. *Bellyband*
13. *Tug*
14. *Girth*
15. *Hames*
16. *Sidecheck*

because the shoulder is unrestricted and the point of traction is correct for optimum efficiency.

A breast collar consists of a heavy leather strip or breastpiece suspended from a neck strap. The breastpiece lies across the chest just below the windpipe and wraps around the forequarters above point of shoulder. Traces are stitched or buckled to the breastpiece. A breast collar can easily be adjusted to fit a variety of horses. The point of traction of the breast collar is lower than that of the neck collar. This fact, coupled with the position of the breast collar in relation to the shoulder, makes it more suitable for use with very light vehicles or vehicles equipped with singletrees.

The length of the traces determines the position of the horse in relation to the vehicle. Usually they are made of leather straps layered and stitched together; heavy-harness traces sometimes are made of chain. Each trace is attached at one end to the collar and at the other end to the vehicle. The size of the horse and the style of the vehicle influence trace length. For example, a longer trace is required for a jog cart than for a surrey. The jog cart has two wheels of small diameter, and consequently longer shafts are necessary to achieve balance. The four-wheeled surrey, on the other hand, is well balanced and its shafts need to be only long enough to accommodate a horse.

The saddle and the pad are the two basic types of leather surcingles designed to circle the heart girth of the driving horse. The saddle is quite substantial and is used when the horse must support part of the weight of a vehicle with its back, as is the case with two-wheeled vehicles. The shafts of the vehicle are supported by open or closed tugs. The open type are leather loops buckled to straps that are attached by metal rings to the side of the saddle; the closed tugs are formed by a continuous leather strap or backband that passes through a channel in the saddle. The backband is more comfortable for a horse over rough terrain, since it allows the saddle to absorb some of the stress of the vehicle's uneven motion. A girth buckles to either side of the saddle under the horse's barrel and holds the saddle in position just behind the withers. Driving girths are adjusted to be slightly looser than riding girths. This allows for some shifting of the saddle which helps dissipate the shocks the horse receives from the movement of the vehicle.

The bellyband is a leather strap with buckles on each end. It passes through a leather keeper on the underside of the girth and buckles to leather straps suspended from the tugs. This apparatus holds the tugs in position, which prevents the shafts of a two-wheeler from tipping upward and dumping its load. Show harness commonly used by breed-ring exhibitors employs another system to solve this problem. This is the wrap strap, a long band of leather that slides through a channel on the outside of the girth. The strap is drawn taut and an end is wrapped around each shaft in front and back of the tugs. The wrap buckles back to itself. This method keeps the shafts from tipping upward and also acts as a brake for light show vehicles, since breeching is not used with this type of harness. Saddles are equipped with bearing-rein hooks, rein terrets, and a ring for the crupper strap. They often are decorated with patent leather.

Pads are much lighter than saddles. Their function is to carry the traces and to provide a ring for the crupper strap. Like saddles, they also furnish a hook for the bearing rein and terrets for the reins and are embellished with patent leather.

The main function of the crupper is to keep the saddle or pad from slipping forward. The crupper strap passes through a dee ring on the saddle or pad and attaches by a buckle or stitching to a dockpiece. The dockpiece, a loop of soft, stuffed leather, fits snugly around the tailhead of the horse. The crupper strap also supplies a slot from which to hang breeching.

Breeching is the means by which the horse stops a vehicle that does not have mechanical brakes. There are two common types of breeching. In each the horse uses its hindquarters to hold back the vehicle. False breeching is the more simple arrangement. It consists of a wide leather strap stretched between the shafts a few inches behind the horse. Full breeching is more customary. Here, a loin strap slips through a slot on the crupper strap and is buckled to a wide band of leather, or "breeching body," that passes around the hindquarters just below point of buttock. A breeching strap is attached to a ring stitched to each end of the breeching body. Each breeching strap can be wrapped around a shaft, threaded through a metal dee, and buckled back to itself. Some breeching is simply passed through the metal dee and buckled back to itself.

The preceding paragraphs describe basic, common parts of harness. There are in addition a multitude of useful training aids that attach to or replace parts of harness, as well as harness for multiple hitches, racing, and other specialized aspects of driving. Each of these areas will be covered in detail in later chapters.

Harness Care

Harness is made primarily of leather, a material with a dual personality. At its best it is strong, durable, and pliant. But like all natural materials, leather is also vulnerable. Heat, moisture, salt, and strain will cause it to dry out, roughen, rot, and eventually crack or tear. Without proper care leather breaks down quickly. However, with consistent attention the same leather can remain strong and supple for decades.

Daily care is the beginning of a sensible program of harness maintenance. Every time you take a harness from its rack to be used inspect the points of stress for signs of wear. Check any parts—such as the billets and tug straps—that bend around or rub against metal fittings. Also examine the pieces that take the stress of draft, that is, the traces and collar. Look closely at metal fixtures—hames, buckles, or rings—to detect signs of rust or fractures. The safety of horses, passengers, and equipment depends upon the ability of the harness to function. If a harness part appears weak, don't take chances. A saddlemaker can restitch or replace leather or metal, but an accident is not so easily resolved.

After use, wipe harness parts with a soft cloth to remove dirt and sweat. Like riding equipment, a harness should be stored on racks that support the pieces so they do not stretch. Rack units are available that have curved braces for the saddle or pad and crownpiece of the bridle. Hang neck collars upside down to keep them from losing their shape. Cotton or canvas drawstring bags can be used to cover the harness; they allow air to circulate which discourages moisture and growth of mold or mildew. They also prevent dust from settling on the equipment and protect the patent leather, which is easily scratched.

An important periodic routine is to take the harness apart and clean it thoroughly with saddle soap. Use as little water as possible and maintain a good lather on the cloth or sponge. A toothbrush and soap can be used to gently clean stitching and other hard-to-reach areas. It is essential to keep the crupper clean. The head of the tail is sensitive and easily irritated by a build-up of dirt or sweat on the crupper.

Dry or cracked leather can be treated with leather oil. Apply the oil generously to the rough side of the leather. Do not oil smooth leather or patent leather. A harness dressing (black or clear) can be used on the smooth side of the harness. These dressings rejuvenate the leather and can be polished to a high sheen, which is essential in the show ring. Patent leather is delicate. It can be cleaned with specially prepared patent leather cleaners. Some household wood waxes (for example, Pledge) also do an excellent job. Or, Vaseline can be gently rubbed onto patent leather and polished to bring out a shine. Always use a soft cloth.

Clean metal parts with products formulated for the specific metal; follow container directions and polish with a soft cloth. Take care not to get these cleaners on the leather. Also, because they are often caustic, they should not be used to clean the mouthpiece of the bit.

The appearance of harness is important. A sparkling harness is an asset in the show ring and a sign of professionalism to other drivers. More important, a clean harness testifies to a program of maintenance designed to ensure safe function of equipment.

The Vehicle

Vehicles were built in amazing variety during the heyday of horse-drawn transportation. Every carriage builder produced uniquely styled vehicles, and individual craftsmen added one-of-a-kind carts and carriages to the array. Today new factories are making competition vehicles and family businesses are engaging in production of cross-country carts, road carts, meadowbrooks, and other informal pleasure vehicles. The range of available equipment—contemporary, reproduction, antique—is astounding.

Although vehicles can differ widely in body design, there are fundamental structural and functional similarities that provide a system of broad classification. For example, the body entrance of a ladies' phaeton has a graceful open curve to accommodate a full and flowing skirt. The body of a spider phaeton is raised on ornamental ironwork. But what *all* phaetons have in common is that they are four-wheeled, informal, owner-driven vehicles. Most vehicles can be categorized by the answers to these two questions: 1. Does the vehicle have two or four wheels? 2. Is the vehicle turned out to be informal (owner- or amateur-driven), or formal (to be driven by a professional coachman)?

Two-wheeled vehicles might be called the economy cars of horse-drawn equipment. They are small, light, and generally less expensive to obtain and easier to maintain and store. They include jog carts equipped with wire-spoked

Ill. 2-7. Dump wagon, circa 1910. (Courtesy/Carriage Museum, Have Mule Will Travel)

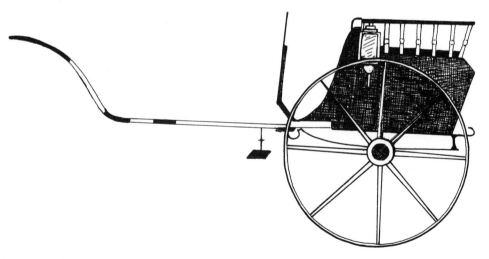

Ill. 2-8. Gig.

wheels of small diameter, as well as more elegant gigs featuring large wooden wheels. Road carts, governess carts, dog carts, village carts, and a number of other types provide more variation in function and style.

Two-wheeled vehicles have several advantages. They are ideal for single horses (in fact, only a few types are considered suitable to be driven Cape

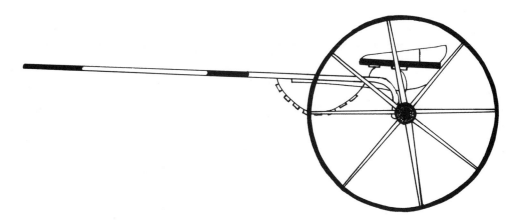

Ill. 2-9. Road Cart.

Ill. 2-10. Breaking cart is designed with long shafts and low center of gravity for safety and stability. (Courtesy/Carriage Museum, Have Mule Will Travel)

or curricle fashion with a pair). They serve well as breaking or training carts because their light weight does not stress a young or green horse. Equipped with a folding seat, one can get in and out quickly. Most important, they follow a horse even when it changes direction sharply. (The undercarriage of a four-wheeled vehicle can lock when executing a sharp turn, causing the vehicle to overturn.)

Two-wheelers are mainly informal town, country, or sporting vehicles.

Ill. 2-11. Jog cart. (Photographer/Joanne Feldman)

Ill. 2-12. Buggy:
  1. Body
  2. Undercarriage

Ill. 2-13. Ladies' phaeton.

Four-wheeled vehicles are more diversified. They encompass the lowly buckboard and buggy and the impressive landau and victoria as well as a varied assortment of intermediate vehicles. A single horse can be put to many of these vehicles but others are intended for multiple hitches. Four-wheeled vehicles have the advantage of larger load and passenger accommodations. Also, the structure of these vehicles allows for better balance; little or no weight bears on the backs of the horses, as it does with two-wheeled vehicles. Many four-wheelers traditionally are driven by amateurs, but this category also includes opulent carriages and coaches furnished with box seats for coachmen. These are the limousines of horse-drawn equipages, intended for formal outings—balls, opera excursions, and state occasions.

All vehicles have two main parts: body and undercarriage. The body is the passenger and load area. The undercarriage consists of the wheels, axles, springs, and forecarriage parts.

Bodies usually are constructed of wood. Formal vehicles always are painted and pin-striped or lined with subtle colors. Black, olive, Brewster or coach green, or burgundy are the most common colors. Informal vehicles can be painted or the natural wood varnished. Country or sporting vehicles often are lighthearted in style, incorporating wicker and bright colors into their scheme. The upholstery (if any) is in keeping with the purpose of the vehicle. Brocade is appropriate for a coach, cotton cord cloth more suitable for a gig.

Wheels are made of a combination of woods, which vary from one locale to another. One wheelwright uses oak for the spokes, elm for the nave (central block), and ash for the felloes (a felloe is a section of the wooden rim of the wheel, which is encircled with a metal rim and into which the spokes are driven—usually one felloe to every two spokes). An iron channel encircles the felloe, and rubber tiring is forced into the channel. Wooden wheels are joined to the undercarriage with axles. Simply described, axles are comprised

Ill. 2-14. Aluminum wheelwright's table. (Carriage Shop/Have Mule Will Travel)

Ill. 2-15. Pit for heating metal rim to 700 degrees before applying to wooden wheel. (Carriage Shop/Have Mule Will Travel)

Ill. 2-16. Machine used to force rubber tiring into metal channel of wooden wheel. (Carriage Shop/Have Mule Will Travel)

of two metal shoulders or arms connected by a metal bar termed the axle bed. The arms pass through the naves of the wheels and are held in place by wheel nuts. The nut is screwed onto the threaded end of the arm. A hub cap covers the nut. Wire wheels, somewhat similar to bicycle or motorcycle wheels, are used on the jog carts, racing sulkies, and viceroys manufactured today. They range from 24 to 28 inches in diameter and consist of a rubber tire supported by a metal rim and spokes. Each is attached to the metal cart frame by a carriage bolt that passes through the hub of the wheel; a nut holds the wheel in place.

In most vehicles the body is suspended above the axles and wheels by a system of springs. Springs are metal plates accurately joined in a variety of patterns including cee-springs, whip springs, and elliptic springs, which are the most common. Elliptic springs, which were invented in 1804, eliminated the need for a perch (a foundation between the front and rear axles), making possible vehicles of lighter, more attractive design. Springs function as a buffer between the wheels and the body, absorbing some of the shock of rough travel.

The forecarriage of a vehicle is composed of several main elements. These

Ill. 2-17. Wire wheels. (Courtesy/Wilform Buggy Works)

Ill. 2-18. Elliptic springs clamped to body framing. (Carriage Shop/Have Mule Will Travel)

Ill. 2-19. Steam-bent shafts. (Courtesy/Wilform Buggy Works)

usually include: front wheels, axle, fifth wheel, futchels, sway bar, splinter bar, and a number of various smaller parts. The fifth wheel is a support and guide that pivots on a pin connecting the body of the vehicle to the forecarriage. The futchels are pieces of wood that bolster the splinter bar, shafts, or pole at one end and the sway bar (a balancing factor for the forecarriage) at the other end. The splinter bar is a crosspiece spanning the front of the vehicle. The traces are attached directly to hooks on the splinter bar; or a singletree is bolted or strapped to the splinter bar and the traces are attached to hooks on the singletree. The splinter bar is the means by which a vehicle is pulled along.

Shafts and poles are the steering mechanisms of carts and carriages. The shafts are two cylindrical wooden rails joined to the futchels of the vehicle to form an open-ended shute between which a single horse is harnessed. Curved shafts are made of steam-bent ash. Shafts also prevent a vehicle from running forward into the horse. They are used with two- and four-wheeled vehicles and sleighs. Pairs of horses are harnessed to either side of a pole. The pole fits between the futchels and is held in place with a pin. Lead bars are attached to the front of the pole for multiple hitches. The pole is sturdy timber reinforced with metal plates. A pole is rarely used with two-wheeled vehicles but is customary for large four-wheeled vehicles and sleighs.

We will return to a more detailed discussion of the traditions and functions of vehicles in later chapters. Now we are ready to introduce the horse to basic equipment and to begin elementary training.

3

ELEMENTARY TRAINING

"An artist trains, other people break." These words of Major H. Faudel-Phillips, in his *Driving Book*, are the perfect introduction to a chapter about basic training. The message can be phrased in many ways, but the meaning is always the same. The most important aspect of starting a horse in harness is the trainer. The value of a trainer is the sum of his or her temperament, experience, and creativity. These qualities may be present in varying amounts, but they all must be present in some degree. A patient temperament, a working knowledge of the fundamentals of harness training, and a flexible, open mind are necessary for success as a trainer.

Ill. 3-1. Ground driving. (Photographer/Joanne Feldman)

The Curriculum

A standard program for introducing horses to the equipment and skills of driving is outlined in this chapter. It is a conservative and painstaking program designed for the novice trainer. It explains the steps necessary to take a young horse—one that is broken to the halter and stands tied—from the pasture through longeing, ground-driving, long-lining, and pulling a drag, to the first few days when he is hooked to the training cart. A span of approximately three months is allotted to accomplish each of the steps in the program.

The following schedule is long and thorough. It has been devised for the untrained horse and novice trainer, who will benefit from practice that would bore their more accomplished counterparts. For instance, a well-schooled saddle horse has already learned to longe and to respond to verbal commands; this horse will require less schooling before being hooked to a vehicle. Also if the trainer is a veteran he or she can take shortcuts. Veterans know from experience how to evaluate the temperament and prior training of a horse and how to deal effectively with problems that may arise. In other words, there is room for improvisation. The following training program should be adapted to meet individual needs.

Longeing

Longeing is one of the fundamentals of training. The simplicity of the maneuver is deceptive when we consider its value as a training tool. Essentially, the horse transcribes a circle around a stationary handler. The handler has a rope to guide and rate the horse, and a long-thonged whip to encourage forward movement. The horse is taught to respond to verbal commands to walk, trot, canter, and halt. Many horse owners use longeing only for exercising their horses, but it has additional uses as a schooling aid that make it relevant to this chapter. It can be used to establish communication and to build confidence between horse and trainer, as well as to bit and balance the horse.

Standard items of equipment for longeing include a halter or longeing cavesson; a longe line, or a tape and chain; and a 6-foot whip with a 6-foot lash and popper. Such traditional items are acceptable for this phase of training, but as an alternative to the line and chain, I recommend a training rope. It is less severe than a chain, less bulky than a halter (fits comfortably beneath the headstall of a driving bridle), and can be tied to the harness saddle when not needed. Also, unlike the customary longe line, the training rope is useful throughout elementary training.

To make a training rope, refer to Illustration 3-2. You will need 30 feet of half-inch sisal/hemp rope, a 3-inch swivel snap, a 1-inch metal ring, a 2-inch pulley, a 12-inch length of small-diameter pliable wire, and a roll of electrical tape. Begin by unraveling and rebraiding the rope to make it soft and supple.

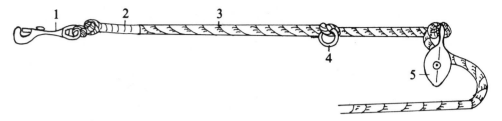

Ill. 3-2.   The training rope:
  1. *Swivel snap*   4. *Metal ring*
  2. *Tape*   5. *Pulley*
  3. *Rope*

Ill. 3-3.   The training rope tied to a halter.

Next, tie the pulley and ring in place. Their positions are determined by the size of the horse's head. The portion of the rope that circles the neck must be long enough to be loose; the section that extends from the throttle, beneath the jaw, to the pulley must be correct to allow for accurate positioning of the noseband.

The following dimensions are for a horse of 14-2 to 15-2 hands. The rope can be retied and should be adjusted to fit the horse. Place the pulley 50 inches from one end of the rope. Knot the pulley to the rope to hold it in place. Tie the ring in position 9 inches in front of the pulley. Tie the snap to the end of the rope nearest the ring. Use 6 inches of rope to tie the snap in place. Bind the knot with wire and carefully cover the wire with a wrapping of electrical tape. At the start of training, the rope is worn beneath the halter, with the noseband loosely tied to the noseband of the halter (Ill. 3-3).

A circular, fenced, training pen 60 feet in diameter is ideal for early longe training. If a pen is not available, use the corner of a larger arena and represent the perimeter of a 60-foot circle with traffic cones or cavaletti or ground poles. These provide a guideline for the horse and are particularly important when blinders are introduced. Also, the trainer will have less difficulty teaching a horse to execute a circle if the horse is aware of the boundary of the circle.

Basic longeing theory suggests that when they are correctly positioned,

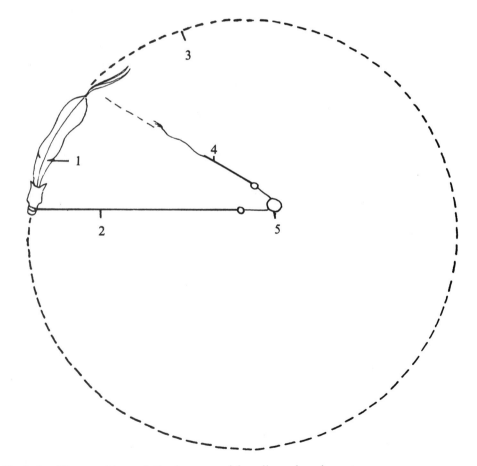

Ill. 3-4. The position of the horse and handler when longeing:
  1. Horse   *4. Whip*
  2. Rope   *5. Trainer*
  3. Perimeter of circle

horse and trainer form a triangle, with the horse as the base, the trainer as the apex, and the rope and whip as the sides. The trainer is not stationary. He or she must maintain a position just behind the heart girth of the horse in order to be effective in encouraging forward movement. Body language is one of the keys to success in longeing. If the horse is moving to the right, the active rope hand of the trainer will be the right hand. The excess rope is looped in the left hand so that it may be released if extra length is needed. The whip is also held in the left hand with the tip pointing downward in the direction of the haunches of the horse. The fingers and thumb of the active hand are over the rope, knuckles up. Move the rope and whip to opposite hands when changing the horse's direction.

Use a sharp, short downward jerk on the rope for corrections. Instantly release pressure so the rope can slide back through the pulley and release the tension of the rope around the horse's nose. Do not exert a steady pull or try to drag a horse with the training rope. The unrelieved tension of a tight rope around the nose is enough to spark a struggle, and in a tug of war the horse will win. Several jerks on the rope can be administered in rapid succession, but always allow a few seconds' release between each jerk. Horses strongly resent unjust treatment, so be sure the punishment fits the crime. If it is harshly or unfairly applied, the rope loses its effectiveness as a training device. One of the basic rules of horsemanship is *know when to quit*. It helps you avoid getting into a struggle of wills with your horse.

If the horse fails to move forward in response to a voice command, the trainer may resort to the whip. The whip is held in the hand closest to the hindquarters with its tip pointed toward the ground until needed. Usually it is sufficient threat just to raise the whip, but occasionally it is necessary to shake the thong or snap the popper. A lazy horse may require the thong brushed across his side or belly to assure him you mean business. However, don't lash the horse across his hocks or hindquarters. Not only will this gesture encourage the horse to kick, it will instill fear of the whip. Respect for the whip is essential, but fear of the whip will limit its effectiveness as a training tool for advanced driving.

An assistant is necessary to start a horse who has had no prior longe training. The assistant (using a short rope snapped to the halter) leads the horse around the circle. The trainer stands in the center and gives verbal commands. Have the horse led at the walk and trot until he begins to understand what is expected, then gradually wean the youngster from dependency on the assistant. Young horses, with their limited attention span, respond better to short, frequent sessions than to long, single sessions.

Regardless of whether the student horse is a youngster or an aged saddle horse, now is the time to begin to teach the language of driving. Verbal communication is vital; it is one of only three aids available to the driver: voice, whip, and bit. Unlike a rider, a driver cannot use body language (the horse is wearing blinders), weight shifts, or leg aids to emphasize a point. It is important to devise a language made up of a few words and sounds, for example; *Ho, Walk, Walk on, Trot, Trot on,* a *cluck* for forward momentum, and a *kiss* sound for an extension. Use *Ho* instead of *Whoa* if you plan to use *Walk;* this will avoid a confusion of "W" sounds. *Come here* is an excellent signal for an upcoming change of direction. Some drivers say *Come right* or *Come left. Easy* or *Whup* can mean "slow down but don't break gait." The exact words are not important, but their consistent repetition throughout the training period is essential.

Don't chat or nag. Words are precious commodities. Each is a direct order, and should be followed swiftly by further encouragement if ignored. Just as a horse can be made dead-sided by a rider's overactive leg or hardmouthed from excessively mobile hands, it can become immune to sounds that are not commands. Everyone has observed the type of driver who clucks with every stride. The cluck elicits no response from the horse; it has become just another background noise. Also remember that horses have an acute sense of hearing. It is not necessary to shout. A low, assured voice is most effective.

The first week of training can be spent teaching the horse to longe and developing a relationship based on mutual trust and respect. The horse will gain confidence as he becomes familiar with your schedule and expectations.

New equipment can be introduced at the beginning of the second week. Start with the saddle. An assistant can stand at the shoulder of the horse holding the lead rope; do not tie the horse. Remove the crupper strap, and lay the saddle gently over the horse's back, positioned behind the withers. Reassure the horse as you loosely buckle the girth. Adjust it gradually. The girth should be snug enough to prevent it from slipping but should not be tight. Depending on the style of saddle, buckle the bellyband or buckle the wraps through the tugs so these leathers do not slap against the horse or drag on the ground. Walk and then longe with the saddle in place.

On the following day, reattach the crupper strap to the saddle. Again with an assistant holding the lead, place the saddle on the horse's back halfway between the withers and tailhead. Gently lift the tail and ease the dock piece of the crupper underneath. Be alert, because a sensitive horse may resent this procedure. Buckle the crupper closed. Move the saddle forward into position and buckle the girth. The crupper strap may follow the curve of the horse's back during early training, but it should not be so long that the dockpiece hangs more than an inch below the tailhead; otherwise it may slide up and down and cause irritation or sores. Hand-walk and then longe the horse. It is a good idea to canter him the first day he wears the crupper. The new and startling sensation of the crupper is particularly evident at this gait. A green horse will often round his back, clamp his tail, and buck once or twice. A sharp correction with the rope coupled with the command *Quit* usually ends the rebellion.

The next step is bitting. Choose a half-cheek snaffle of moderate diameter for the young horse. It should not be so narrow that it pinches the lips nor so wide that it hangs over the sides of the mouth and breaks at the joint. Have a harnessmaker wrap the mouthpiece with undyed chap leather, stitched in

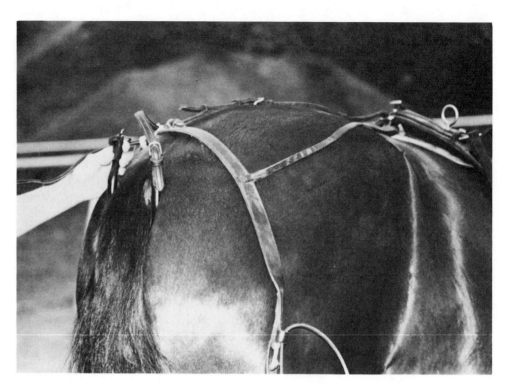

Ill. 3-5.   Buckling the dockpiece of the crupper.

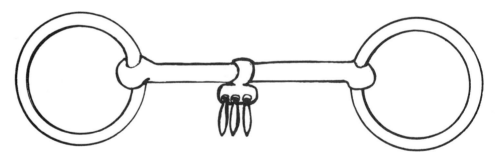

Ill. 3-6.   Mouthing bit with keys.

place. Hang the bit on an open (no blinders) headstall. Adjust the headstall so that the bit is slightly lower than normal in the horse's mouth. Introduce the bit with a few kernels of grain. The leather, grain, and lowered bit will encourage the horse to play, chew, and suck the mouthpiece. All these devices help the horse accept the bit. This is a crucial step in training, because a good harness horse must be prepared with a trusting mouth for the constant light contact necessary when driving.

An older horse who has been bitted for saddle work may be fitted with a mouthing bit, which is a mild bit equipped with keys. A mouthing bit will relax a tense mouth and to some extent soften a hard one. It may be intro-

Ill. 3-7. The training rope and bridle:
1. *Training rope*
2. *Long-lines*
3. *Tie to hold cheek pieces of bridle in place when a cavesson is used instead of a noseband*
4. *Leather strap to hold training rope in position*
5. *Cavesson*

duced with grain and hung low in the mouth, as described above. If you object to feeding a bitted horse, the same effect can be obtained with a toy squirt gun. Spray a stream of water into the horse's mouth to encourage salivation.

To prepare the horse for longeing, put on a loosely buckled cavesson, the training rope, the headstall, and the bit. The noseband of the rope is held in place with a leather strap buckled around the browband (Ill. 3-7).

After two or three days of longeing with bit, saddle, and crupper, the horse can be introduced to bit pressure via side reins. Side reins are two straps made of leather or leather and elastic. One end of each strap buckles to the bit ring, and the other end hooks to the saddle. The side reins are adjusted gradually until the horse can be longed with steady pressure on the bit. Their function is two-fold: to accustom the mouth of the horse to contact, and to teach the horse to balance when the movement of the head and neck is restricted, as it will be when driving. On the first day the side reins are loosely adjusted and don't come into play unless the horse pushes his nose far forward, raises his head high, or hangs it very low. Each day adjust the reins until there is light contact on the bit when the horse is traveling with a normal head carriage—flexed at the poll, nose a few inches in front of a vertical line (an imaginary line at a right angle to the ground, a few feet in front of and parallel to the chest of the horse). Do not yet tighten the side reins beyond this point. This would create the false impression of a finished headset, when in fact the horse is strapped into a position which he cannot maintain without their assistance until he is more muscled and better balanced.

Simultaneously with training in side reins, the next piece of equipment—blinders—may be introduced. It is not necessary to set up a harness bridle for the first few lessons. A blinker or blinder hood can be used over the training bridle. It is best to introduce blinders in a familiar enclosed area. An assistant should be on hand to steady and restrain the horse. Carefully put the hood on the horse, covering first one eye and then the other. It is important to allow the horse frontal vision out of one eye at all times when putting on or taking off the hood. When a horse is wearing blinders, take care to speak to him as you approach and before touching him. The horse may be frightened even by a friendly pat if he can't see it coming. Once the hood is in place, have the assistant lead the horse around the pen. It is reassuring to the horse to follow the assistant and later the rail or perimeter of the circle until he becomes accustomed to having his vision restricted. The trainer may take his position in the center of the longe area and give the familiar commands. When the horse appears to have accepted this new piece of equipment, the assistant can step out of sight and longeing can proceed as usual.

The blinders are a major step in harness training. The horse is asked to depend upon the trainer to an extent not common to saddle horses. Take the time to be sure he is confident and controllable.

Every day of the horse's first week in blinders, and in conjunction with regular longeing sessions, spend a few minutes leading the animal outside the ring. Begin this phase of training in well-known territory, and if the horse is not skittish gradually venture into less familiar areas. For the sake of discipline, be sure the horse is wearing the training rope on these outings.

Each horse learns at its own rate of speed. However, at the end of a month the average, previously untrained young horse (who has been worked five or six times a week, approximately 40 minutes a day—two 20-minute sessions for young horses) should be wearing the saddle, crupper, bridle, bit, and blinders. This same horse must also be confident and responsive when longeing. It is most important, though, that the horse be obedient. If he does not respect the behavioral boundaries you have set for him, take more time and do not proceed to the next phase of training until he is compliant. This does not mean you have to browbeat the horse into submission; simply be certain that he understands your commands and respects your ability to enforce them. The future success and safety of a horse in harness is determined to a great extent by this early foundation.

Ground-Driving and Long-Lining

Ground-driving takes place when the trainer, equipped with two long reins or long-lines hooked to the bit, follows behind the horse (Ill. 3-1). When the horse is similarly outfitted and transcribes a circle around the trainer, it is termed "long-lining." Both training techniques are used to teach the potential harness horse to maneuver in response to the commands of a handler who is some distance away.

A set of lines is required. These may be 25 to 30 feet long and constructed of substantial leather, rope, or webbing with a swivel snap attached to one end. Leather and web long-lines are available in some tack stores. Cotton web dog tracking leads (purchased in pet shops) can be used if they are at least ¾-inch wide and the snap is sturdy and small enough to fit through the rein terrets on the saddle. Also, snaps can be attached to lengths of rebraided sisal/hemp rope and used for lines.

To begin training to ground-drive, equip the horse with saddle, crupper, training rope, and open bridle. There is more than one school of thought regarding the use of blinders during the initial ground-driving sessions. Some trainers prefer, as I do, that the horse be able to see the handler, whip in hand,

Ill. 3-8. Long-lining. (Photographer/Joanne Feldman)

Ill. 3-9.   Training a young horse to ground drive.

following behind. There are two reasons for this. First, if the horse can see the whip, he will be less frightened when touched by it (providing the animal is not whip-shy due to mishandling); also, the horse will be more respectful of a trainer who has a whip. Once this training is initiated, the blinders can be reintroduced.

The long-lines are hooked to the bit, but again there is more than one successful theory as to the best route to the bit. Some trainers prefer to thread the lines through the rein terrets, or the tugs, on the saddle before hooking them to the bit. On the other hand, lines hooked directly to the bit have an additional function as a training aid. For the first few sessions they can be drawn along the barrel and haunches to encourage an uneducated horse to turn.

As before, a helper is necessary to handle the training rope. The trainer holds a line in each hand. The line comes from the bit and enters the front of the hand between the index and middle finger. The thumb is pressed against the line on top. The remaining fingers are closed over the line (see Ill. 4-6). The excess line is looped and hung over the little finger of the right hand. Neat loops are a must to ensure easy lengthening of the lines if necessary. Lines dragging on the ground can be dangerous (Ill. 3-9).

Put the lines on the horse for the first time inside an enclosed area. Station an assistant at the horse's head and drape the lines across the animals back and hindquarters. Most horses, being accustomed to handling and grooming, do not resent this procedure, but some youngsters are startled enough to buck or kick and should be corrected with a sharp tug on the training rope. It may take several sessions before a timid horse ceases flinching when a line is draped over his hocks, but be persistent; the horse should stand quietly regardless of where the lines touch his body. A harness is comprised of many flapping leather straps, and a horse must be desensitized to their effect before he is safe to hook and unhook.

To continue, the assistant may walk beside the horse, if necessary, guiding him around the perimeter of the pen. The trainer follows at a safe distance behind the hindquarters, holding the lines and whip. He or she should give the now familiar verbal signals for walk, halt, stand, and eventually trot. The trainer walks or trots in unison with, though behind, the horse. Maintain a steady, equal, light contact on the lines. When you trot, be careful not to transmit the motion of your body through your hands to the horse's mouth. Just as when you are riding, your hands must be independent of your body.

When the horse is relaxed, executing gaits and transitions on the rail or perimeter of the circle, begin exercises off the rail. A horse is on the rail when he can follow it, using it as a guide for his movements. Shallow serpentines and changes of direction across the center of the circle will introduce the horse to the weight of the long driving lines, the pressure of the driver's hands, and the whip as an aid; they also help to stretch and supple the muscles. Signal an impending change of direction with a verbal cue. I say *Come here*, but any consistently used term will do. In the beginning it may be necessary to guide the horse into the turn with a leading rein. A trainer employs a leading rein when he moves one hand and arm away from his body and by exerting greater pressure on one side of the bit, draws the horse's head in a specific direction. However, if the horse is on the bit, it is more sophisticated and efficient to release the tension on the outside line and let the inside line draw the horse into the turn. The whip may be laid gently along the outside of the hindquarters to encourage the horse to follow his head and neck around the turn and to discourage counterflexing. Counterflexion occurs when the head and neck of the horse bend in one direction and the barrel and hind-quarters remain straight or point in the opposite direction.

A horse that moves straight forward is the aim of every driver. A straight horse follows the prints of his front hooves with the prints of his hind hooves. If he is transcribing a circle, both sets of tracks follow the same perimeter. The trainer instills and polishes these qualities during sessions of ground-driving and long-lining by means of correct reining procedures, use of the whip to move the haunches, and suppling exercises.

Forward movement is the hallmark of the obedient horse. Obedience should be established during longe training and reinforced in this second stage of schooling. If the horse does not move forward from a verbal command followed by a cluck, flick the lash of the whip against his barrel where the leg of the rider would contact his side. Do not slap the whip across the hind-quarters of the horse. This is an invitation to a kicking spree.

A well-balanced driving whip, 60 inches long, with a drop lash of sufficient length to reach the shoulder of the horse, is ideal for ground-driving. A longe whip is suitable for long-lining, but its length, lack of balance, and excessively long lash make it an awkward tool when ground-driving.

Once the horse understands what is expected, replace the blinder hood or driving bridle and thread the lines through the terrets on the saddle before hooking them to the bit. At this point the assistant should become invisible and remain quiet, out of sight, carrying the training rope. His or her only function now is to apply instant correction during moments of extreme disobedience so the trainer does not have to use the bit for punishment. Begin ground-driving outside the ring. One word of caution: don't drive a green horse wearing blinders through narrow gates, doorways, passageways, or between parked cars. His response to the aids still lacks refinement, and unexpected contact with an unseen immovable object will frighten him.

Simultaneously with ground-driving, long-lining can begin inside the 60-foot training area. To start, the assistant leads the horse around the perimeter as the trainer moves to the center of the circle. The outside line is drawn gently around the hindquarters to guide the horse. Once the horse is responding steadily to commands, the assistant may stand beside the trainer. This requires some teamwork; trainer and assistant have to move together to avoid tangling ropes and bodies. After a few sessions the reins should be threaded through the terrets on the saddle and the horse equipped with blinders.

Long-lining is a versatile training technique. The trainer can watch his horse perform and still have access to all driving aids. The position recommended for the trainer in longeing is also correct for long-lining. The method described for holding the lines when ground-driving remains the same. Maintain a light, constant contact with the bit. Avoid holding the horse on the rail with the outside rein or dragging him around the circle with the inside one. The horse should be "between the lines," on the bit, balanced, and straight. Use the rope for corrections. Once the lesson is learned, the horse may be long-lined in open areas.

At this point, evaluate the effectiveness of the bit you have been using. If the horse is leaning on the bit and is heavy and unresponsive to your hands, the leather can be removed from the youngster's bit; an older horse can be fitted with a half-cheek snaffle having a mouthpiece of medium diameter. Some

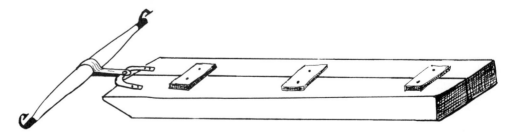

Ill. 3-10. A drag.

trainers recommend introducing the liverpool bit (reins buckled in plain cheek position) at this stage of training.

The average young horse will require several weeks of ground-driving and long-lining before he is ready to pull a drag. He should move forward eagerly, halt and stand quietly, and change directions fluidly. In essence, he must be obedient and maneuverable before he can advance to the next stage of training.

The Drag

The green horse who is steady and responsive when ground-driven is ready to learn to pull an object. Every trainer has his or her own device for this stage of training. Some use a plow with the blade set deep; others, a tire and chain; and still others, a railroad tie. Whatever is used, the drag must be heavy and awkward to pull (to discourage runaways) and difficult to break. A knowledgeable trainer with several carts at his disposal can afford to skip this stage, but for safety of horse and equipment, it is a wise precaution to devise a drag and have the horse pull it on several occasions in a variety of situations before you hook him to a cart.

The drag illustrated (Ill. 3-10) is constructed of two 6-foot lengths of landscape timber (6-inch by 6-inch by 6-inch lengths of creosoted wood used to keep garden soil in place) nailed together with crosspieces; the front end is beveled for smooth going over rough terrain. A horseshoe is nailed to the top of the front piece, and to this the singletree is attached by means of a carriage bolt. Pieces of chain, with double-ended snaps at their opposite ends, are attached to the trace hooks of the singletree; the length of chain depends upon the size of the horse. The snaps at the end of the chain are hooked to the traces. The horse, in draft, must be far enough in front of the singletree to avoid hitting the drag with his heels as he moves. This type of drag is usable only on level ground; it would slide into the horse on a grade.

Prepare the horse to pull weight the day before he is hooked to the drag. After a routine ground-driving or long-lining session, remove the lines, put on the neck or breast collar, and attach a kicking strap to the crupper strap. (A kicking strap hangs over the haunches and buckles around the cart shafts. Its function is to discourage kicking in harness, since the horse must lift the cart to get his hindquarters off the ground. In this instance it is used as a trace holder.) Buckle the kicking strap so a loop hangs on either side of the horse. Run each trace through a saddle tug and a loop of the kicking strap. Snap a 6-foot lead rope, or similar sturdy rope equipped with a snap, to the end of each trace. The assistant holds the end of a lead in each hand and follows behind, positioned well out of kicking range, as the trainer moves the horse forward. The traces will rub and flop, but sessions of long-lining should have accustomed the horse to this sensation. The assistant should gradually pull, exerting increasing pressure against the traces, as the trainer encourages the horse to keep moving. After several circuits of the ring the assistant will be skidding along on his heels. When the horse is pulling the drag, the traces will hang low around his hocks and may rub against his hind cannons when he changes direction; in preparation, the trainer has to simulate this situation while urging the horse to continue forward. If the horse submits quietly to these proceedings, he may be hooked to the drag on the following day.

For the initial hooking, choose an enclosed area, at least twice as large as a 60-foot training circle. A larger enclosure provides the safety of confinement yet eliminates the need for tight circles or sharp changes of direction. At the end of a session of long-lining, neatly fold the lines over the crupper strap and lead the horse to the drag. Allow him to inspect the new piece of equipment, then ask your assistant to move the drag, first in sight and then behind the blinders, to accustom the horse to the sound. Next, stand the horse parallel to the rail and position the drag directly behind. The assistant must be at the horse's head, holding the training rope, while you hook the traces to the snaps on the chains. Never leave a horse partially hooked. Hook both traces in quick succession. A startled horse can be controlled if it jumps forward with both traces hooked, but the same horse half-hooked to a drag or cart will panic as the vehicle swings sideways.

Ill. 3-11. Picking up the lines.

Ill. 3-12. Pulling the drag.

Once the horse is securely hooked, the trainer can pick up the lines and whip and move into position behind the drag. The trainer should give the command to walk while the assistant, remaining in front of the blinders, leads the horse forward. The horse may hesitate as it moves into draft, but a little encouragement is usually sufficient to keep him moving.

Many horses adopt a strange posture when they first pull weight. They carry the head and neck unnaturally low and struggle along on the forehand. After two or three sessions they learn to engage their hindquarters and push against the collar.

The first drag-pulling session can be short. If the horse pulls the drag at a walk and trot and executes a gradual change of direction (after the assistant has moved behind the blinders), unhook. On the following day, expect the horse to spend the entire training session hooked to the drag. At the end of the third lesson, leave the ring and conclude the session in the open. Once the horse has pulled the drag six or eight times, proceed to the next step. The drag is heavy, awkward, and noisy. By comparison, the cart is light, smooth-riding, and quiet. If a horse is steady and responsive pulling a drag in familiar and less well-known environments, the cart will seem easy to him.

The Shafts

Shafts sometimes present a problem. Most horses accept confinement between the shafts, but there are always those few who bump against a shaft the first time and swing away only to bump against the opposite shaft, and a frenzied side-to-side struggle ensues that usually results in a broken shaft. To avoid this event, there is one more step to follow before hooking the horse to the cart. Trainers who routinely start horses in harness keep a set of *detached shafts* on hand as a training device. These shafts are fitted into the tugs for support and are carried behind by an assistant while the trainer moves the horse around to accustom the animal to their restriction. For those without an extra set of shafts, a simple travois can be built that consists of two long, light poles and a crosspiece. The poles are put through the tugs and held in place with wrap straps. Their opposite ends drag on the ground behind the horse. Usually one session of dragging poles is enough to convince a horse to tolerate the shafts. The horse wears the complete harness with the exception of the reins. The trainer exercises control with the training rope during this procedure.

The Cart

The day the horse is hooked to the cart will be uneventful provided he has been patiently introduced to the equipment and carefully schooled to master the fundamental skills of driving. Two helpers who are experienced with hooking procedures should be on hand to assist. Put the full harness on the horse, including a kicking strap (instead of breeching), a loosely adjusted checkrein, and the training rope. Use long-lines instead of reins for this initial session. Place the cart in the center of a large fenced arena (a two-wheeled jog cart or a specially equipped breaking cart generally is used). Long-line the horse in this environment until he is relaxed. Then introduce him to the sight, smell, and sound of the cart. Ground-drive around the ring as an assistant pulls the cart in front, beside, and behind the horse. If he accepts the sound of the cart when it is out of sight, he is ready to hook.

Stand the horse in the center of the arena at an angle to the rail with the long-lines easily accessible, folded over the crupper strap. Once hooked, you should be able to drive onto the rail in an easy, curved line, without taking any corners that might cause the shafts to poke into the shoulders of the horse. A familiar person should be stationed at the horse's head. This assistant will stand directly in front of the horse, holding the looped training rope and loosely grasping the lines on either side of the bit. A tense grip on the lines must be avoided by the assistant; it causes the snaffle to pinch the lips and also communicates a sense of unease to the horse. However, do be firm. Days of training have been devoted to teaching this horse to stand. It is a reasonable request.

The initial hooking procedure should be done smoothly and quickly. The trainer can hook the left side so that he or she has easy access to the lines and the second helper can hook the off side. To begin, each must take hold of a shaft and draw the cart to the horse. Gently but firmly say *Ho*, lay a hand against the buttocks, and draw the vehicle forward. Guide the shaft tips

Ill. 3-13. A horse correctly positioned in relation to the vehicle. (Gayle Warren driving the Arabian stallion, Mon-Bo).

through the tugs. The tips should be at point of shoulder and the tug strap should hang parallel to the saddle. The handler and assistant simultaneously thread the traces through the leather loops on the shafts and attach them to the trace hooks, which are on the ends of the singletree or screwed to the inside of the shafts. Traces are correctly adjusted if the shaft tip is at point of shoulder when the horse is in draft. The shafts should be nearly level and should follow the line of the traces. Raise or lower the tugs to achieve this adjustment. Next, position the tug straps so they hang parallel to the saddle, and buckle the bellyband or wrap the wrap straps. If you use a bellyband (since we are not using a breeching), be sure the cart is equipped with tug stops, metal projections on the underside of each shaft that prevent the shaft from sliding through the tug and the cart from running into the horse. Wrap the wrap straps around the shafts, in front and back of the tugs, to hold them in position (Ill. 3-13). Don't wrap the traces against the shaft. They should hang loose, between the horse and shaft, encircled by the leather straps of the wrap or bellyband. The wrap provides efficient braking for a light, two-wheeled vehicle on level ground, but don't try to go downhill without the added security of thimbles (cups of leather that fit over the tips of the shafts and are attached by a leather strap to a dee ring on the saddle) or breeching.

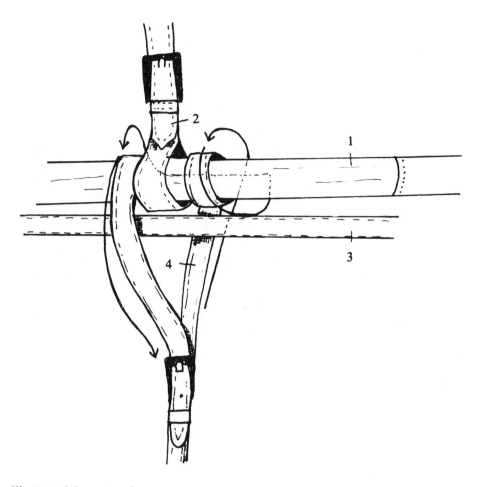

Ill. 3-14. Wrapping the straps:

   1. Shaft   *3. Trace*

   2. Tug   *4. Wrap strap*

Last of all, hook the kicking strap (Ill. 3-14). A kicking strap is a handy safety device when properly adjusted; it must never be so tight that it interferes with the natural movement of the hindquarters. If so, it may cause the vice it is designed to prevent.

The horse is hooked. After a visual check of the equipment, the trainer should take the lines and move into position behind the cart. Post an assistant on each side of the cart. The helper holding the training rope must be on the inside. This assistant, upon hearing the trainer give the command to walk, should lead the horse forward. The trainer can follow behind the cart the first time around the ring, or stand on the back step, if there is one—although most knowledgeable trainers agree that the safest and most effective place for the driver is in the cart. If the horse is steady after the first round or two, the assistant can step back behind the blinders, forcing the horse to rely upon the driver.

After circling the arena several times, change direction across the diagonal.

Ill. 3-14A. "Putting up" the lines can refer to storing the reins or long lines on the harness while the driver is busy hooking or unhooking. The lines must be shortened (reins require one fold—roughly in half; long lines must be looped several times because of greater length), then slipped between and folded over the top crupper strap. The keepers on the crupper strap can be pushed against the lines to hold them in place.

This movement is an important test. For the first time the cart will shift, causing the shafts to press against the sides of the horse. One assistant can take hold of a shaft and gently pull in the direction of the turn. The outside shaft will press against the barrel of the horse and ease the animal around the turn. This is more effective than pulling the head and neck around (and often into the tip of the shaft) with the training rope or reins. After circling several times in the new direction the horse can be asked to trot a few strides with the rope-holder jogging along beside. Next, walk into the center of the arena and halt. The helper with the rope, called the "header," should stand at the horse's head, following the same procedure as when the horse was hooked. The trainer can "put up" the lines and, with the aid of the second helper, proceed to unhook. "Put up" the lines by folding in half the length of reins extending from the rein terrets to the driver's hands. Grasp the center of the fold and slide the lines between the two pieces of the crupper strap. Fold the lines in half again, draping this half over the top crupper strap piece, with the excess lines dangling on the left side of the horse. In an emergency, a single tug pulls them free. Unhook the traces first. They should be tied in loops that

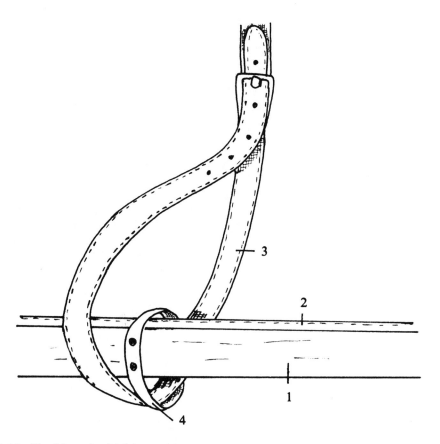

Ill. 3-15. Hooking the kicking strap.

do not drag on the ground. Next, unbuckle the kicking strap. The ends of this strap should be threaded through the keepers. Unwrap the wrap straps or unbuckle the bellyband last. The tips of the wraps should be threaded through their keepers so they hang in neat loops from the girth. Next, push the shafts out of the tugs. Do not let the cart fall. Raise the shafts above the back of the horse and instruct the header to lead the animal forward.

On the second day, replace the long-lines with leather driving reins and follow the same procedure. The third day, if all is going well, the assistant holding the training rope can ride in the cart with the driver. After four or five days the rope can be dispensed with, although the assistant should be on hand to act as a header when hooking and unhooking.

An arena is an excellent safety and training resource, but riding rings of traditional size are restrictive for the driving horse. If you are lucky enough to have access to a fenced track, wean the horse from the arena and drive him on the track as soon as possible. If he has been ground-driven and has pulled the drag on the track, this can be accomplished by the second week. If available, quiet roads and wide trails offer good practice for the green harness horse. Be cautious and take an assistant and the training rope on the first session on the track and on the first few outings outside the enclosure. Do not let the length and breadth of the cart make you stiff and awkward.

The third time the horse is hooked begin the suppling exercises—shallow serpentines, circles off the rail, and figure eights—learned in long-lines. A harness horse, as evidenced by the spectacular dressage and obstacles tests routinely performed at the world driving championships, can be a very handy animal.

Next, before delving into advanced driving disciplines and techniques, a word about the driver.

4

THE DRIVER

When you picture a masterful driver you might envision a man or woman conservatively dressed in a contemporary style, wearing a small hat, gloves, and a lap robe or apron. Whip in hand, the driver sits with back pressed into the seat rest, feet braced against the floorboards, elbows close to sides, hands strong and quiet, holding reins taut as guitar strings. With eyes steadfastly directed over the backs of the working horses, this driver is shrewdly capable of judging pace and distance. The horses are dressed in clean, well-fitted harness, and the vehicle is rattle-free and immaculate. The horses are attentive. They carry their ears cocked rearward,

Ill. 4-1. Mavis Clarke of Willaston Hall in Cheshire driving a pair of Lippizzan geldings to a Bennington phaeton on the obstacle course at Bicton in Devon, England. (Photographer/Ian Brooke, Brooke Photographic)

funnels for the driver's every word. And they are steady on their bits. They move willingly into their collars as they thrust with conditioned hindquarters against the load. The groom sits like a statue, expressionless and assured, as the vehicle rumbles rapidly on its way.

It is obvious from this portrait that the driver—or, as traditionalists say, "whip"—must be adept at many things. A good driver must understand the traditions and skills of driving and be competent in executing them. He or she must be qualified to evaluate the condition of the equipment on a daily basis and be able to maintain a long-term program of upkeep. And perhaps most important, a good driver has to be able to fulfill the role of "captain" of his or her turnout during the drive. In this capacity the driver must be able to make instantaneous, intelligent, and responsible decisions. This particular assortment of qualities could explain why driving, until recently, was thought to be a sport for affluent, middle-aged men of above-average education and/or intelligence.

Attire

The attire of a driver is a facet of equipment, and standards are dictated by reasons other than fashion. Attire is first of all functional; it is an aid to performance of the task at hand. The basic driver's outfit calls for a conservative jacket and trousers or skirt, a hat, gloves, sturdy shoes or boots, and in most instances an apron or lap robe.

Neat, conservative dress is preferred because it is efficient, visually appealing, and to some extent safer. Driving today is not a fashion parade or an attempt to relive the past. It is a viable contemporary sport in which the trappings of period costumes and contemporary high fashion would be out of place. Such clothing is discouraged for practical reasons as well. Floating veils or scarfs, dangling ties or belts, voluminous skirts, and excessive jewelry can become tangled in the equipment or flap in the breeze and frighten a neighboring horse.

Color *is* a matter of tradition. Subtle, earthy tones (browns, grays, deep greens, burgundy, and natural blues) are considered proper. A correct color is one that closely matches the coat color of the driver's horses or a part of the vehicle, such as the upholstery or body color.

The type of event determines the quality of the outfit. An expensive wool suit is reserved for the presentation section of a combined driving event or the turnout class at a major show. Comfortable cotton slacks or jeans are appropriate for schooling along a country road. Any outfit that limits agility, however attractive it may be, is inappropriate. A driver needs roomy clothing.

Comfort is also a consideration. Linen or cotton suits can be kept crisp and trim and are cool during the warm months of the year. Cord cloth suits

Ill. 4-2. Patricia A. James, a masterful driver, driving Pebble Bay to a ralli car.

are smart and provide an alternative for brisk weather. Wool is ideal at all times. (Information about suits for specialized driving events—breed, combined, racing, and liveries for antique carriages—is included in later chapters.)

The function of a driver's hat is obvious. It keeps the head cool in summer and warm in winter. The brim shields the eyes from the sun. A suitable hat is small, narrow-brimmed, and close-fitting. For esthetic reasons, the color should be compatible with the rest of the turnout. Large hats, floppy brims, long feathers, droopy ties, scarfs, or ribbons do not make fitting headgear for drivers.

A driver uses his or her feet to brace against the floorboards to achieve a firm body position. For this reason shoes or boots should be sturdy, with a substantial sole and some system of ankle support. Loose-fitting, awkward shoes are impractical around horses. No high heels or sandals please, and certainly no bare feet.

Gloves protect the hands of the driver. They prevent the reins from abrading or blistering the skin as a result of the consistent, firm contact required when driving. They also make possible a more secure grip of the leathers. As a rule of thumb, driving gloves should be one size larger than what is normally worn to allow for adequate finger movement when holding a handful of reins. A medium-weight leather is best. A glove of natural, woven

Ill. 4-3. Bill Robinson, internationally successful driver of Hackney Horses and Ponies and American Saddlebred Horses.

fabric (cotton or wool) should be substituted or worn over the leather gloves when driving in fog, rain, or snow, since moisture makes leather slippery.

The apron and lap robe are traditional pieces of equipment whose purpose is to keep harness black, dust, and mud off the driver's suit. Generally, an apron is a rectangle of fabric that buckles, ties, or buttons around the driver's waist and covers the driver's clothing from the waist to the tops of the shoes. A lap robe, or rug, is large enough to cover both driver and passenger and provides warmth as well as protection. A variety of materials—ranging from linen in summer to fur in winter—are used for aprons and rugs. An all-purpose apron can be constructed of two layers of fabric: waterproof fabric on one side and a conservative tartan plaid or check fabric on the other side, bound together with several rows of decorative stitching. An apron must be wide and long enough to be comfortable and to cover the driver.

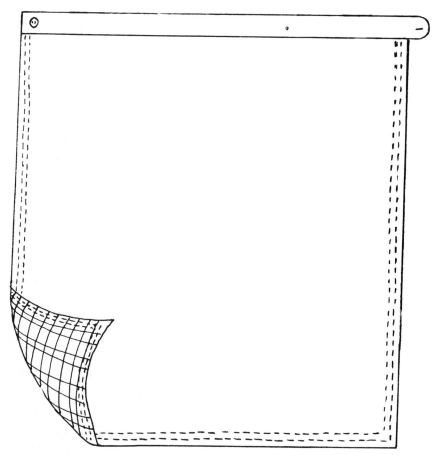

Ill. 4-4. A driving apron.

Some form of eye protection is generally worn by drivers of low vehicles like jog carts, sulkies, or viceroys; without them a faceful of dirt could blind a driver at a crucial moment. Clear eyeglasses, sunglasses, or driving goggles (available in tack and racing-supply stores) should be part of everyday driving attire.

Position

The position of the driver, like the seat of a rider, is his or her foundation. A firm, strong position relates directly to how well the driver is able to direct and hold the horse or horses. Correct position involves the whole body. Hands receive a lot of attention and they are an important aid, yet they are only one aspect of position. Hands should be held close together at waist level, several inches in front of the body, supported by supple wrists. Arms are carried bent at the elbows with upper arms held parallel to the sides. Arms held out in front of the body appear tense and tire easily.

Ill. 4-5. Correct driving position. Driver, Pat James.

Rating the horse needs strength from the back and shoulders as well as from the hands and arms. To be effective, the shoulders must be straight and the back upright, supported by the seat rest. If you doubt this, try an experiment. Drive forward for a few strides in a hunched posture, then readjust your position and drive with straight, firm back and shoulders. The second position is distinctly more comfortable and efficient.

Finally, the hips and buttocks need to be firmly pressed into the seat, with the legs (knees together) and feet braced against the floorboards for security. A passenger can grab hold of a part of a vehicle as it lurches over a bump, but the driver doesn't have this advantage. HRH the Duke of Edinburgh, in his book, *Competition Carriage Driving,* recommends that the driver wear a large, loose belt over his clothing that can be grabbed by a groom if necessary to hold the driver in his vehicle. But a groom is a luxury unavailable to the majority of drivers. Most have to depend upon seat, legs, and feet—in other words, on the firmness of their position—to keep them in the cart.

The Aids

Aids are devices used by drivers to communicate with their horses. The horse's obedience to the aids is established over a period of time through careful training. The use of aids is emphatic with a green horse and becomes increasingly subtle with advanced schooling, until mere signals are enough to elicit a preconditioned response from the finished horse. The driver has access to three major aids; hands, which communicate via reins and bit to the horse's mouth; whip; and voice.

Hands

A driver's ability to communicate with his hands to the mouth of the horse is elementary to successful driving. It is the means by which a driver balances the horse, rates speed, effects transitions of gait, and initiates changes of direction. George Morris, in his book, *Hunter Seat Equitation*, divides hands into four categories—bad, "no," good, and educated—that can be applied equally well to drivers. Bad hands are rough, unyielding hands that inflict pain. "No hands" drivers have failed to understand that consistent contact is the essence of driving; they punish the horse's mouth with constant interruptions of contact. Good hands are light, steady, and elastic. Educated hands belong to the virtuosos of the harness world; these drivers communicate to their horses with the subtle craft and skill of accomplished artists.

Hands should be held at waist level, wrists approximately 3 inches in front of the body and 10 inches apart. An expert reinsman will not move his hands outside an imaginary 12 square inches of space.

There are two correct ways to hold the reins for singles and pairs. Horses that are expected to show animation, brilliant high action, or speed in harness usually are driven with a rein in each hand (Ill. 4-6), as are young horses still wearing snaffles and horses in situations where greater control is required (for example, the marathon section of a combined driving event). A rein passes between the forefinger and middle finger of each hand and is held secure with pressure from the thumb; the whip is held in the right hand. The excess, or bight, of rein coming from the left hand may be carried over the little finger of the right hand to keep it from dragging behind the cart or becoming tangled in the spokes or over the little finger of the left hand, where it does not interfere with the whip.

To shorten the reins, take the right rein between the middle and ring finger of the left hand. Both reins are now in the left hand, although the bight is still in the right hand. With the right hand, pick up both reins in front of the left hand. The right rein is held between the forefinger and middle finger, and the left rein between the middle and ring finger of the right hand. Draw the reins to their desired length through the right hand with the left hand. Take the left rein with the left hand and move the hands apart. To lengthen

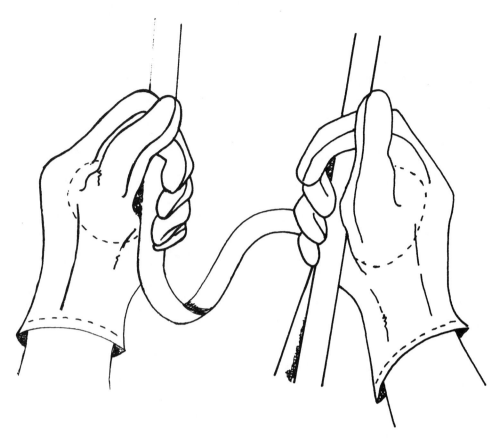

Ill. 4-6. The reins held in two hands.

the reins, slide the hands along the lines. If correct contact is maintained, changes of direction are initiated by moving the outside hand forward, releasing contact on the rein opposite the direction of the turn. The remaining contact on the inside rein guides the horse around the turn.

Antique carriage enthusiasts generally drive with both reins in the left hand and the whip in the right hand (Ill. 4-7). These drivers desire a balanced, forward-moving horse who displays a natural self-carriage and relaxed attitude. In this case, the left rein passes over the forefinger, and the right rein is carried between the middle and ring fingers. The thumb points to the right and does not press against the reins. The middle, ring, and little fingers hold the reins securely against the palm of the hand. The reins may be shortened by either of two methods. Place the right hand over the reins several inches in front of the left hand, taking the left rein between forefinger and middle finger and the right rein between the ring and little finger. Push the reins back through a relaxed left hand. Or, use the right hand to pick up the reins behind the left hand and reposition the left hand on the reins.

There are three methods for signaling a turn.

(1) The horse can be asked to turn with the aid of the right hand. A right turn is signaled by placing the right hand on the right rein a few inches in

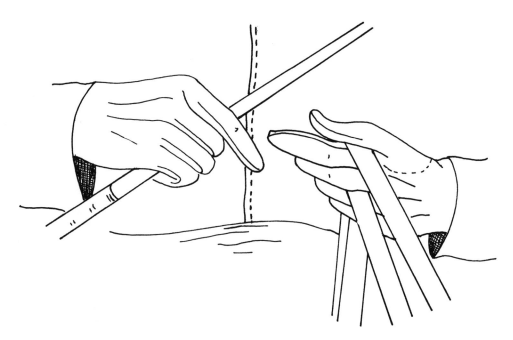

Ill. 4-7.   Two reins held in one hand.

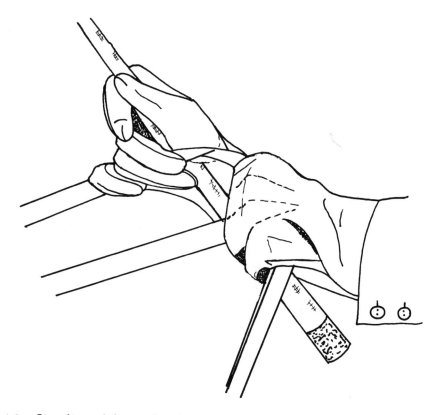

*Ill. 4-8.   Signaling a left turn by placing the free hand in front of the hand holding
the reins.*

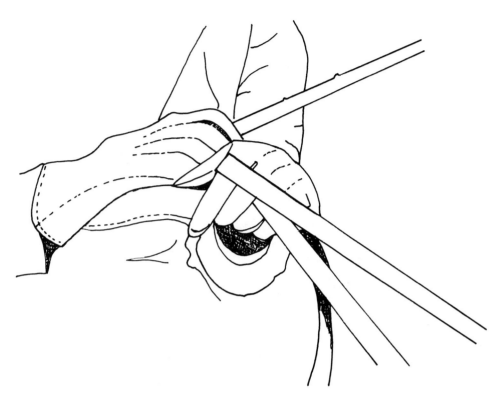

Ill. 4-9. Signaling a right turn with the left hand only.

front of the left hand. A slight pressure is exerted downward and to the rear. This same pressure used by the right hand on the left rein signals a left turn.

(2) A turn also may be initiated by the left hand only. In this instance a left turn is cued by turning the hand clockwise and slightly to the right, tightening the left rein and releasing pressure on the right. To turn right, the hand is turned counterclockwise and moved to the left, tightening the right rein and releasing contact on the left one.

(3) A last method of turning requires taking a loop of rein. A left turn is signaled when the right hand grasps the left rein with the middle, ring, and little fingers, several inches in front of the left hand. The left rein is pushed back by the right hand until a loop is formed and held in place under the left thumb. To initiate a right turn, conversely, the right hand feeds a loop of right rein to the left hand. The loop is released as the turn is accomplished.

A steady, balanced contact with the mouth of the horse is more important to successful driving than the manner of holding the reins. Maintaining correct contact with the mouth of a harness horse requires that the driver's hands be dexterous and sensitive. The following exercise can be used to gain an understanding of the subtleties of contact. Tie equal lengths of rope to the ears of a straight-backed kitchen chair. Sit in a similar chair facing the back of the tied chair. Take a rope in each hand, or both in the left hand, and attempt to balance the lead chair on its back legs.

(Rein handling for multiple hitches is discussed in later chapters.)

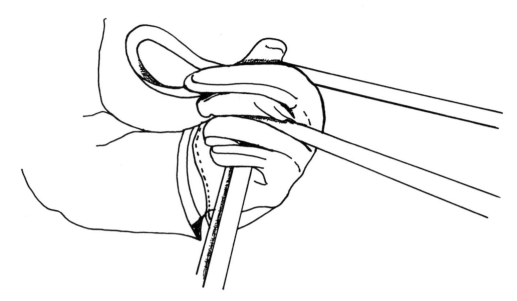

Ill. 4-10. Signaling a left turn by taking a loop of rein.

The Whip

The whip is a tool that consists of a stick, a leather-covered handhold between the metal end cap and metal ferule or collar, and a thong attached to the tip of the stick that ends in a lash or popper. A driver should carry a whip in his or her hand at all times during a drive. It is used to encourage forward movement, to move the hind or forequarters of the horse, and to regain its attention after a distraction. The whip will become ineffective if used routinely to express a driver's displeasure.

The whip is held in the right hand at a right angle across the body. It is usually grasped where the handle joins the ferule. The handle passes through the closed hand and rests against the thumb muscle. It is important that a whip be properly balanced and thus light and easy to hold in this manner. An unbalanced whip is a burden to carry and awkward to use.

Traditional whips are made of flexible hollywood and sport a leather thong held in place by a goose-quill tube, that is bound to the tip of the stick with black thread. They are ideal for turnout classes and presentations, but their fragility and expense make them a luxury. Leather-bound driving whips with a fiberglass core do the job equally well besides being inexpensive and durable. Driving whips should not be left standing in a corner. Because of their length and construction, this treatment could cause a whip to develop a bow, and a bowed whip is unattractive and difficult to use. Store driving whips in a rack that supports their entire length. Holly whips shold be kept hanging on a whip reel.

The same whip is not correct for every turnout. The stick and thong should be long enough for the driver to be able to flick the lash against the shoulder

Ill. 4-11. Teaching a horse to move away from the whip during a ground-driving session. Pat James driving Little Owl.

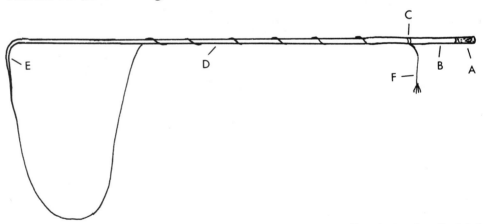

Ill. 4-12. A whip with a folded thong. A-Cap; B-Handle; C-Ferule; D-Stick; E-Thong; F-Lash.

of the horse farthest from him. Thus, the whip used for a single pony is shorter than that used for a single horse.

To request forward movement, the driver uses a flick of the lash against the shoulder, side, or belly of the horse. Slapping the haunches of the horse is an exhibition of poor whip-handling and a provocation to kicking. To ask for lateral movement, the stick of the whip can be laid gently against the quarters. A touch with the lash of the whip also brings the attention of a distracted horse back to the driver. Response to the whip should be taught during ground-driving and long-lining sessions. The horse should have learned to react to the whip positively, without fear, before he is hooked to the cart.

The thong of the whip is folded or "laid-up" around the stick when the driver is not using it. This gives a neat appearance and keeps the lash out of the face of the passenger. The thong is wrapped around the stick in a counterclockwise direction (Ill. 4-12); one large loop hangs from the tip while many tight loops twine down the remaining two-thirds of the stick. The end of the lash is held in the driver's hand. The driver lets go of the lash and points the stick downward to unwind the thong and prepare the whip for use.

Voice

The voice is a versatile aid. It can be used to soothe or to encourage, to instill confidence or to scold. Much information about the use of a driver's voice is included in chapter 3, "Elementary Training." A driver's voice should be low and assured yet capable of modulation to show pleasure or displeasure.

Ill. 4-13. A few reassuring words encouraged this frightened horse to move forward and relax.

A driver's vocabulary should be consistent, concise, and economical. Always use the same word to signal a certain gait or movement. Don't add a string of adjectives; the horse doesn't understand and the sounds may be confusing. Don't repeat a command once the horse has obeyed, otherwise it will lose its value as a signal. *Do* use verbal praise. Horses need to know when they are doing well, and most respond with enthusiasm to your approving sounds.

Judgment

Judgment is the ability to form an opinion, make a decision, and act responsibly, wisely, and authoritatively. It is a composite skill and requires patience, a lack of bias, good sense, discretion, knowledge, and confidence. A driver is expected to exercise judgment in many areas before, during, and after a drive. He should inspect the equipment to be sure it is in a sound state of repair before the drive. He must check to make sure the horse or horses are correctly hooked. It is also the driver's job to be forearmed with a knowledge of the horses he is driving on a particular day. He must know their temperament, training, level of ability, and condition, and ask no more nor accept any less from the horses than these facts dictate. During the drive the driver must be able to predict how his equipment will perform and be able to make quick decisions regarding width, turning radius, and balance.

Ill. 4-14. Judgement. Antoni Musial driving for Poland at the 1982 World Driving Championships. (Photograph/Courtesy of Driving Digest Magazine)

After the drive, it is his responsibility to see that the horses are properly cooled down, groomed, and "put up," and that the vehicle is stored and the harness cleaned properly. In other words, a driver must be a jack-of-all-trades, combining elements of knowledge proper to a mechanic, coachbuilder, harness-maker, horse trainer, physicist, ship captain, and business manager. The best school for honing judgment is experience. An aspiring driver should spend much time driving under supervision and/or riding with other drivers.

5

PLEASURE DRIVING

orming the backbone of the driving community are the people who drive
for pleasure. These individualists do not need the thrill of competition
or the prospect of a roar of spectator approval to convince them to pull
the vehicle from its shed and bring the horse in from the field. The majority
of them are newcomers who have not yet acquired a taste for competition,
although a great many are longtime enthusiasts who prefer a private drive
to any other aspect of the sport. They are not as vocal as the dedicated competitors or as public as the professional trainers, but as the subscription lists of
driving organizations and magazines attest, they are everywhere. The act of
driving—the view across the back of a horse, the smell of leather mixed with

*Ill. 5-1. Lady Jane Watkin-Williams driving her double dog cart through the Italian
Garden at Birton Manor in Devon, England. (Photographer/Ian Brooke, Brooke
Photographic)*

that of seasonal foliage, the sound of wheels crackling over the road in unison with hoof falls, the motion of the vehicle and the feel of the reins—is the source of pleasure for this special group of drivers. And the drive, be it an hour's jaunt along a rural road to sample the glories of autumn color or a brisk jingling ride in a cutter with a friend, is its own reward.

The Pleasure-Driving Horse

The pleasure-driving horse is a specialist whose attitude and training prepare him to be steady, confident, and mannerly in harness. He is expected to trot along roads and accept the company of cars and trucks. Dogs bounding through bushes and children riding noisy toys and bicycles must not faze him. On cross-country excursions he will face mud, water, swinging branches, herds of cattle, and partridge thundering from beside the trail without showing any serious disobedience. He must be able to accept guidance from uneducated hands and, since he is often a "backyard horse" used only for weekend and holiday drives, he is expected to remain well-mannered with only infrequent exercise. He needs to be surefooted on slippery pavement and rough trails and fit enough to pull a loaded vehicle over long distances. The ideal pleasure horse combines an array of natural traits, abilities, and learned skills, and that makes him, like every specialist, a rare individual. But most horses

Ill. 5-2. A pleasure-driving horse.

have the necessary qualities which can be encouraged or developed with the right care and schooling.

Special Care

Anyone who owns a horse must be aware of the animal's unique needs and keep the horse prepared for the work he is expected to perform. At times you will need to emphasize different aspects of basic care in order to keep a specialized harness horse tuned for his job.

Weight is the first consideration. A fat horse or an underweight horse is unhealthy; neither can be expected to perform up to its potential. Several factors affect the amount of nutrients necessary to keep a horse at the right weight. The animal's rate of metabolism and the amount of work performed on a given day are important indicators. An average horse doing light work can be expected to thrive on good quality hay or grass, a vitamin-mineral supplement, free-choice salt, and fresh water. A horse who is driven for an hour two or three times a week is doing light work, but his physical appearance is the best guide to the adequacy of his diet. Increase or decrease the amount and change the type of feed when necessary. If there is any question, a veterinarian is probably the best source of advice, since feeding is an individual matter for each animal. Make changes gradually, however. The equine digestive system is simple and does not readily adjust to sudden dietary changes. This fact applies especially to a grass diet, because the amount and quality of grass is seasonal in most areas. Introduce a horse slowly to a diet of spring grass and wean him gradually from grass in the fall.

Horses, like all athletes, require regular workouts to reach and maintain fitness. It is not reasonable to expect a horse to pull a vehicle a long distance once a week without some program of conditioning exercise between drives. Longeing and long-lining sessions are less time-consuming than an actual drive and can fill this gap. Start an unfit horse gradually. The initial session can be as short as fifteen minutes and be limited to walking and trotting. Over a period of days, slowly increase the overall length of time as well as the length of time at each gait. Don't overlook the walk. This is an important conditioning gait when it is done in brisk, ground-covering fashion; it is not of much value when the horse is allowed to weave sleepily around the circle. At the end of a sensible six-week program the average horse should be able to work steadily for forty-five minutes without stress. Once conditioned, a horse does not sustain condition without regular workouts. In fact, condition begins to diminish slowly after five days without exercise. Conditioning procedures (geared for competition) are discussed at length in chapter 8, "Combined Driving."

Most horses require exercise to remain eventempered as well as fit. Attitude and training are secondary to good spirits when a horse that has been

Ill. 5-3. Ground-driving sessions can keep a horse fit.

stall-bound for several days is hooked without benefit of a warm-up period. Twenty minutes on a longe line provide an outlet for pent up energy. Start with five minutes walking to warm up, and follow this with a period of alternating gaits—walk-trot-canter-walk, with the length of these periods determined by the condition of the horse. Turning a horse loose in a large enclosure after several days without exercise is unwise. He will take the "edge" off, but the joy of freedom may cause a flurry of exuberant activity that could stress or injure stiff, cold muscles. A controlled warm-up is safer. Ideally, a horse who can't be exercised daily should be kept in a paddock or pasture that is equipped with a shelter. The daily sights, sounds, and activity of roaming a field supply diversion and exercise.

Unshod hooves, periodically trimmed and balanced, are best for the pleasure-driving horse who must travel on pavement as well as on trails. The natural grip and expansion of the unshod hoof provide security on both asphalt and natural terrain. Smooth metal shoes are slippery on pavement. If shoeing is necessary because of an unhealthy hoof wall or tender soles, there are ways to increase traction at the same time. The farrier can insert borium plugs in the bottoms of the shoes. These rough, metal projections give the horse an added grip on asphalt, cement, and ice. There is a disadvantage, however, in that borium plugs bring the hoof to a sudden jarring halt, unlike the

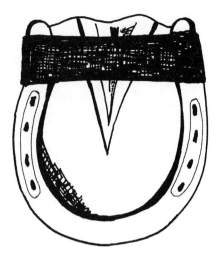

Ill. 5-4. A rubber strip can be attached across the back of the shoe for traction.

gradual shock-absorbing action effected by the natural or smooth-shod hoof, and the sudden jar stresses the structure of the leg. For this reason, borium is not recommended for long periods of time. Some farriers can make threaded holes in the shoes, allowing the borium chocks to be screwed in place for the drive and removed afterward. This also ensures that the front legs won't be injured in the pasture or stall should the horse overreach when he is not wearing protective boots. For workouts or drives, always boot up a horse that is equipped with borium-plugged shoes.

Major Faudel-Phillips, in the *Driving Book*, offers another suggestion for improving traction: nailing a narrow strip of rubber tire across the heel of the shoe. Horses with tender soles, or horses who travel regularly over rocky trails and suffer from bruised soles, may be outfitted with pads. The

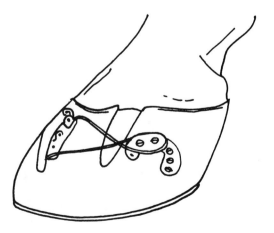

Ill. 5-5. A hard rubber boot covers and protects the whole hoof.

trouble with pads is that they cover the frog and interrupt the natural flow of air, providing a perfect environment for bacteria and predisposing the frog to thrush. Hard rubber boots, available at tack stores, offer an alternative to shoes and pads. They cover the entire hoof and buckle or snap securely in place. The rubber boots can be used when needed, allowing the frog to be uncovered part of the time.

Special Training

The pleasure-driving horse is a performance specialist. So, beyond promoting his attitude and fitness, the driver must provide him with some schooling in unique skills.

First and foremost, a pleasure-driving horse must be patient. Most pleasure horses are owned by private persons who do not have an assistant available to help with hooking before a drive. It is difficult, even unsafe, to hook a

Ill. 5-6. A horse ground-tied, one method of teaching a horse to stand.

horse who refuses to stand quietly without a header. Therefore the horse must be taught to stand quietly, or "ground tie."

This education can begin during grooming. Equip the horse with a halter, chain, and lead. Run the chain through the left ring of the halter, and along the chin groove and snap it to a ring on the right side of the halter. Drape the lead rope over the withers so it is accessible. Command *Ho* and begin a normal grooming session. If the horse moves, repeat *Ho* and reinforce the command with a quick jerk on the chain. Insist that the horse stand throughout the session. An additional command of *Stand* can be given in conjuction with *Ho*; some trainers prefer a separate term for an immobile period following the actual halt. Continue this training during longeing. Put on a halter and the training rope described in chapter 3, "Elementary Training." If the horse does not obey the verbal command to *Ho and stand*, follow with a sharp downward jerk on the rope. Insist that he stop and stand quietly for increasing lengths of time. The word *Ho* is the most important command; he is not ready for hooking until he understands and respects this command.

Support this training during actual hooking procedures by putting the training rope on the horse beneath the driving bridle (Ill. 3-7). Ask an experienced friend to hook the horse while you stand out of sight, behind the blinders, holding the rope. If the horse moves, command *Ho* sharply and follow instantly with a jerk on the rope. One such session is usually sufficient, but if the horse shows signs of regression, repeat the lesson. If you are adept, you can hold the rope in one hand (the hand closest to the horse's head) and hook without assistance. Follow the same procedure for unhooking. The rope can be tied to the saddle during the drive. Don't make it so short that it interferes with normal head and neck movement or so long that it can become wrapped around a shaft. To prevent the latter, it is a good idea to thread the rope under the hanger strap of the breast collar or through a ring on the neck collar before tying the excess to the saddle.

A spooky horse is frustrating to drive and is dangerous as well. A horse who leaps sideways on slippery pavement or runs backward into the path of an uncoming car or over an incline is not a suitable pleasure-driving horse. There are several kinds of spooks. A horse may spook to evade work, or as an expression of high spirits, or because he is frightened. In all but the last instance, spooking is a disobedience. The horse must learn that it is unacceptable behavior. Ground-driving is an excellent means for reschooling a spooky horse. Equip the horse for ground-driving with the training rope beneath the driving bridle. An assistant will be necessary to carry the rope; this person should remain out of sight. Ground-drive the horse along a familiar route that features some of the objects—trash cans, mail boxes, paper bags, or whatever—that cause him to spook. If he appears ready to jump sideways, order *Quit* in a firm voice. The assistant is forewarned and must furnish instant punishment with the rope if the horse does spook. Several lessons may be necessary to change this behavior pattern.

A horse who shies out of fear requires different handling. Most often

Ill. 5-7. Horses are companionable animals. A timid horse will accept and take confidence from the companionship of a dog.

Ill. 5-8. Backing. To perform this movement successfully, the horse must flex at the poll, engage the hindquarters, and respond to a steady pressure on the bit.

this horse lacks confidence. Consistent driving is the best cure. Patiently expose the animal, with an assistant at his head to offer encouragement and lead him past unfamiliar objects. The family dog can be an excellent companion, providing diversion and a familiar reassuring figure for the horse to follow. Avoid roads with traffic until the training program has proved successful.

A pleasure-driving horse should be able to back and sidepass in harness. These maneuvers may become necessary at any time on a cross-country drive if, for instance, a washout or a fallen tree blocks a trail. Both movements can be taught during ground-driving sessions.

A horse is prepared to back when standing quietly. He should be relaxed but attentive on the bit, flexed at the poll, with the hindquarters engaged.

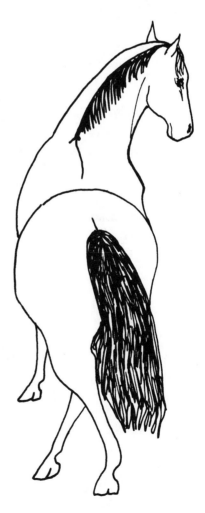

Ill. 5-9. A horse learning to sidepass to the left. The horse is asked to bend in the direction opposite to the movement.

Position an assistant in front of the horse. Command *Back* and exert a steady, equal pressure on the bit. The assistant can push against the chest of the horse to encourage movement. As soon as the horse takes a step to the rear, release pressure, release bit pressure after each step, and command *Ho*. Expect only one or two steps on the first day, but become more demanding as understanding increases. The backing movement should be straight. If the horse moves his haunches out of line to either side, use the whip to tap him into position. The driver's hands, via equal pressure on the lines, keep the head, neck, and forequarters straight.

The sidepass is a lateral movement. The horse does not move forward or back, only to the side. Position the horse facing a fence or wall. Bend his head and neck away from the direction of the sidepass. Give a verbal command—for instance, *Side*—and coax the horse with a leading rein in the direction of the sidepass. In other words, gently apply pressure to one side of the bit, drawing the horse's head in the direction of the movement. Lay the whip against his haunches on the opposite side. It may be necessary to tap the haunches with the whip to encourage him to move away from it. Bending the head and neck puts the horse off balance and in a position to move laterally. The leading hand moves the forequarters and the whip moves the hindquarters. Be patient. Expect only a few steps in the beginning and praise any lateral move even if it is disunited. The sidepass is a difficult maneuver for both horse and driver. Allow the horse to relax and walk along the rail after every successful few steps. It takes several months to teach a horse to sidepass.

The pleasure-driving horse should have sound working conformation, a good disposition, patience, confidence, and basic harness training. Registration papers are not necessary. Older horses—ex-show horses or trotters—with some additional preparation, often make excellent pleasure-driving horses. Be sure to drive a candidate outside an enclosure before making a decision as to whether the horse is capable of this simple but specialized performance.

Equipment

Many pleasure drivers choose antique vehicles. Quite often they become involved with the vehicle first and the horse later. A four-wheeler purchased on a whim during an auction or estate sale can be an introduction to the harness world. Surreys, buckboards, and doctor's buggies are the most common pleasure vehicles. They have much in their favor. Aside from evoking wonderful nostalgic images, they provide room and comfort for passengers and usually come equipped with a hood or cover to keep out sun and rain. Thus, an unelaborate four-wheeled vehicle makes an excellent conveyance for picnic drives or family excursions.

Simple four-wheeled vehicles, in original or partially restored condition, can be acquired at reasonable prices. Many were built as recently as the 1920s or 30s. They are not rare. One that has been kept in storage, protected from

Ill. 5-10. A two-seated wagon.

the effects of weather, usually needs only minor restoration to make it serviceable. It is a good idea to have a coachbuilder appraise the condition of a vehicle.
He will know the points of stress. If there are rusted metal fittings or cracked
or broken shafts, axles, spokes, or felloes, they must be replaced before the
vehicle is used. Luckily, it is no longer difficult to obtain parts. The recent
upsurge of interest in driving has sparked a rebirth of the carriage industry.
Even obscure vehicle parts can now be ordered from a variety of suppliers.
A list of some carriage works, coachbuilders, and wheelwrights follows the
text. More information about these sources can be obtained from the British
Driving Society and the American Driving Society (see Appendix). Some
information about carriage restoration is covered in chapter 10.

Antique four-wheeled vehicles do have limitations for drivers of single
horses. Their size and weight make them taxing for small single horses, especially when they are loaded with passengers and gear. They were designed primarily for travel along packed earth roads, and so little consideration was given
to balanced structure for maneuverability, or to the sturdy construction
necessary to avoid breakdowns during off-road drives.

The demand for wooden two-wheeled vehicles has increased steadily as
the driving community has become more sophisticated and more concerned
with performance than with nostalgia. Two-wheeled carts, despite their limited

Ill. 5-11. A surrey.

passenger space, are more versatile for single horses; meadowbrooks, road-carts, village carts, and wooden-wheeled jog carts are a few of these excellent all-purpose vehicles. They make good road vehicles as well as efficient cross-country equipment. And, as an extra bonus, they are easy to transport. A pick-up truck can convey a two-wheeled cart, whereas a flat-bed truck is necessary to move most types of four-wheeled vehicles.

It is important that a two-wheeled vehicle be of the correct proportion and fit for the horse. A cart cannot be balanced if it is too low or too high for an individual animal. The weight is less significant than the balance. A heavy, well-balanced vehicle is easier to pull than a light but shaft-heavy vehicle that presses down on the back of the horse. Ideally, the shafts should "float" in the tugs. Find this position or point of balance and adjust the harness (by raising and lowering the tugs) to hold the cart in place. The point of balance will be different when there are passengers in the vehicle. Be sure the cart is balanced for the number of people who plan to go on the drive.

Low two-wheeled carts do not make good cross-country vehicles. The first disadvantage is that the driver's view is blocked by the body of the horse; observing traffic and negotiating rough terrain is difficult without an overall view. Also, lightweight wire wheels are impractical for cross-country. Bouncing into a rut will bend a rim and a foray into a bush can snap spokes, rendering a wheel useless.

Ill. 5-12. A two-wheeled vehicle called a "tonga."

Ill. 5-13. Two-wheeled carts can be transported in a pickup truck.

A well-made working harness is a good choice for pleasure driving. It should be constructed of sturdy yet supple leather and be decorated with a minimum of patent leather (which is easily scratched in rough going). Most such harnesses come with a breeching, a necessary piece of equipment for cross-country driving, which is full of surprises, including an occasional steep grade. A sidecheck rein is a good idea, since even the best-mannered horse is apt to grab for a mouthful of grass when walking across a lush meadow. The check should be loosely adjusted to allow the horse normal use of his head and neck and should come into play only when the head drops low. If the harness has rein terrets on the neckcollar or on the hanger strap of the breast collar, then a sidecheck is not essential.

The Drive

The drive may be a casual affair or a vacation planned far in advance. Many drivers find endless pleasure in exploring old logging roads through nearby woodlands, or sightseeing along roads closer to home. Other drivers enjoy a periodic drive along a scenic route far from familiar territory. Many obtain permission from private property owners. Meanwhile, local, state, and federal government agencies are encouraging horse sport and recreation on public lands. Many parks have areas with roads, trails, and often corrals designated for use by horse owners. Departments of Commerce can supply information about such facilities as well as maps of the trails. Horse organizations are another source of this information.

If possible, inspect the route of a planned drive over new ground. Areas accessible to saddle horses can be unsafe for harness horses. Avoid confined, precipitous trails, deep water, and quicksand.

A picnic stop is necessary to rest the horse and refresh passengers on a long drive. Carry a flake of hay, water in a plastic bottle, and a bucket (unless you know you will have access to fresh water for the horse). A halter and lead and a cooler or loin rug are indispensable equipment and should be carried on every cross-country drive. In the event that a breakdown makes delay unavoidable, the horse can be unhooked and, if sweaty, covered with the cooler while repairs are being made.

During a picnic stop, unhook the horse from the vehicle. Remove the bridle, reins, and collar. Loosen the girth one or two holes (but never so loose that it is in danger of sliding sideways), and buckle dangling straps to the saddle or breeching. Don't tie the horse to the vehicle. Choose a sturdy tree or post, and use a quick-release knot (Ill. 5-14). The rope must be long enough so that the horse is not too closely restricted, which could make him panic, but not so long that it can tangle around the legs. If the horse is accustomed to hobbles he can be kept close at hand with this aid. *Never* leave a horse unattended and hooked to a vehicle. Provide the horse with a hay bag or some form of familiar food so it won't feel the need to forage on strange weeds,

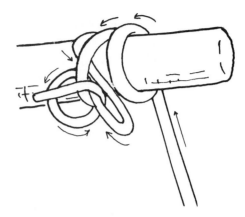

Ill. 5-14. A quick-release knot.

Ill. 5-15. An ear net keeps insects out of the ears during cross-country drives.

plants, and parts of trees. Horses are not equipped with the instinct to avoid all poisonous plants.

Fly repellant should be part of the travel kit. Some areas, especially the deep northern woods, have swarms of persistent biting insects at certain times of the year. A horse in harness is particularly helpless to defend itself against their attack. An ear net, constructed of cheesecloth, offers some protection. Always use an ear net if the wool has been clipped out of the ears. The pleasure-driving horse is better left with its ear hair unclipped. A thorough application of insect repellant also will help. For those who are reluctant to spray poisons on their horses, there are repellants on the market composed of natural, biodegradable ingredients. Follow container directions.

Always carry a hoof pick. A stone can lodge in the frog groove during the drive. If it presses against this sensitive area the horse will be suddenly, painfully lame. Once the stone is removed, if the frog has not been bruised, the horse will be sound.

Almost every drive presents an obstacle or hazard to test the training of the horse and the nerves of the driver. It may be as trifling as a cat scrambling in dry leaves or as serious as a trace snapping at a fast trot. A calm driver is the most efficient hedge against complicating any mishap. If the horse bolts forward, restrain the impulse to pull back. Allow him the freedom and security (remember the flight instinct) of a moment of forward movement before asking him to "pay attention" and slow down. Execute a repeated, firm pull against the bit followed instantly by a brief release. A horse can brace against and effectively ignore a steady pull on the reins.

Ill. 5-16. A driver must be able to read the body language of his or her horse. (Photographer/Joanne Feldman)

A driver should learn to read the body language of the horse. If the animal suddenly pauses, tenses, cranks his head to one side, and points stiff ears in the direction of an unusual sight or sound, this alerts the driver that the horse is preparing to wheel around or jump to one side. A command to walk will distract some horses, as will a shake of the bit; others respond to a flick of the whip on the side. Horses can be reluctant to confront an object they distrust while at a slower pace, yet be confident when trotting briskly past the thing.

It is important to know when to use the whip. For instance, if a horse travels a familiar route without incident and suddenly, on three successive days, stops to stare or backs away from a harmless thicket, then the horse is developing a bad habit. If he was allowed time to reassure himself of the innocence of the bush on the first occasion and continued the drive, it is safe to assume that the behavior has become a means of evading work. Compliance must be required, and the driver's commands supported, if necessary, with a rap from the whip. A less experienced driver can ground-drive to the spot and correct the horse without the encumbrance of the cart. Cease discipline the instant the horse complies.

In most states horse-drawn vehicles have the right-of-way on public roadways, although the majority of motorists are unaware or do not heed this rule. Horses and carts are required to observe traffic laws, which includes giving recognizable hand signals. Stay as far to the right as is safe and obey traffic signals and road signs. Be polite. If the road is narrow, causing traffic to line up behind the cart, move off the road at regular intervals and allow the motorists to pass. Be wary. Some drivers honk, wave, or lean out car windows to shout friendly greetings. Other motorists show displeasure at having to share the road by roaring past the turnout. Both kinds of behavior can be disturbing to the horse and dangerous for other motorists.

Don't drive a horse on a road until he has been introduced to the sights, smells, and sounds of traffic. Begin at home. Ground-drive in the vicinity of a stationary car, then turn on the engine; eventually move the car and ground-drive the horse beside it. Finally, ground-drive along the shoulder of a trafficked road.

Broken equipment is another hazard faced by the pleasure driver. Even careful monitoring can fail to detect a broken buckle or a hairline crack that will pop or give way when you are far from home under the stress of rough terrain. Be prepared to make emergency repairs. Always carry a kit containing a spare rein, trace, leather punch, wire, rawhide, wire cutters, knife, screwdriver, small hammer, and—when applicable—a spare hame strap. Most equipment failures can be temporarily shored up or reinforced for the drive back to the barn.

Two last words of advice. First, follow the time-honored cavalry dictate: walk the first mile out and the last mile back. The first mile of walking warms up cold muscles and the last mile cools heated muscles. Second, control the urge to trot on the return. The open road is a wonderful place to

Ill. 5-17. Driving on a public road. D. Howland driving a four-in-hand of Dartmoor geldings at Cricket St. Thomas, England. (Photographer/Ian Brooke, Brooke Photographic)

teach a harness horse to maintain a strong trot, but the rule of knowledgeable drivers is to trot out and *jog back* to avoid eliciting barn-sour behavior.

After the Drive

The horse is the first concern after the drive. Take time to walk him until his respiration is normal, then bathe, brace, towel, or groom (depending on the weather) until the animal is cool and dry. Return the horse to a clean stall or paddock.

Next, wipe the harness clean and dry. Apply a harness dressing if the leather was soaked during a water crossing or a rainstorm. Hang the harness on a rack, covered with a harness bag.

If the vehicle is muddy or dusty after the drive, it can be washed and sponged clean. Don't use abrasive rags or cleaners, which tend to scratch paint and varnish. Thoroughly dry the wood and leather with soft, absorbent toweling. The leather should be treated with a conditioner before the vehicle is put away.

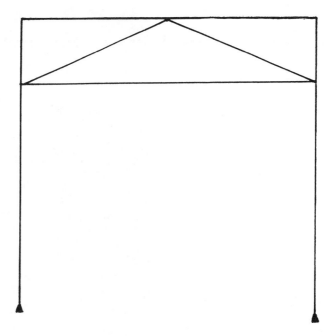

Ill. 5-18. A metal shaft rack is used to keep the shafts of a two-wheeled vehicle off the ground during storage.

Store the vehicle in a shed or building protected from direct sunlight, heat, and dampness. Store cushions in plastic bags with moth balls (camphor) to prevent rodents from nesting in the upholstery. Don't leave the shafts of a two-wheeler resting on the ground. Use a shaft rack, which can be purchased at carriage supply shops, or a padded sawhorse as a rest. In a building with a high ceiling, two-wheelers can be stored with the shafts pointing skyward. The vehicle rests tipped on the seat and springs. Place a pad underneath to protect the paint or varnish, and chock the wheels to prevent rolling. Store hooded carriages with the hoods open to keep the leather from cracking. Cover the equipment with a dust sheet if sunlight enters the storage area through windows.

Winter Driving

The curvaceous sleigh elicits more romantic and lighthearted associations than any other horse-drawn vehicle, images of one-horse cutters speeding across the snow, or of large, coachman-driven sleighs moving with stately grace along plowed roads. For some reason, perhaps in response to the bracing atmosphere and the increased leisure time afforded to rural people during the winter months, sleighmakers of the past abandoned discretion and painted sleighs in bright, frivolous colors, even decorating bodies with fanciful pastoral scenes. Bells, although functional (to warn other drivers of a sleigh approach-

Ill. 5-19. A hooded vehicle, such as this cabriolet, should be stored with the hood up.

ing) add a sparkle of gaiety to every turnout. Sleigh riders complete the picture, wrapped in warm coats and muffs and snuggled beneath sumptuous fur rugs.

Sleighs are commonly made of oak or maple. The frame is steam-bent to achieve the graceful curved lines of the body. Boards are used for the floor and seat. Wood panels attach to the frame and fill in the sides, dash, and back. The runners, also of steam-bent wood and occasionally braced with iron, fit into a metal shoe. Small sleighs are set high, with a single runner on each side. They are awkward to turn and notorious for dumping their occupants into the snow. Large sleighs feature double, or "bob," runners. The two in front are attached to the pole or shafts, allowing for more balanced turning. Sleigh shafts often are offset so the horse can follow in the path of packed snow made by the runners of previous sleighs.

Sleighs are readily available and inexpensive, so pleasure drivers in northern climates don't have to give up driving when snow blankets the trails. Winter driving does, however, require some special forethought. Cold metal freezes to moist skin, and the bit will freeze to the gums and lips of the horse if it

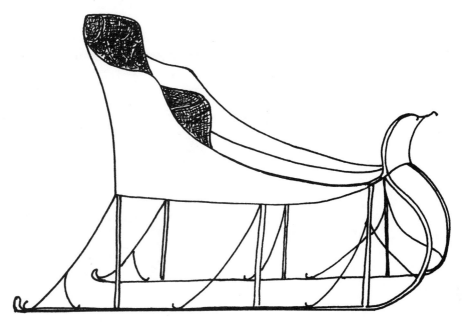

Ill. 5-20. A cutter.

isn't warm. For this reason, the driving bridle should be stored in a heated
tack room or inside the house until it is placed in the horse's mouth. Ideally,
a winter bit should be wrapped in natural chap leather (like the bit described
in chapter 3 for starting a young horse) and equipped with leather cheek guards
to keep the metal from touching the lips or gums of the horse. The crupper
also must be warm before it is placed against the sensitive, hairless skin beneath the tail. And, the horse should be barefoot, or be shod with shoes or
equipped with boots that increase traction on ice and slippery surfaces. Be
alert. Snow can pack in the frog groove and freeze into a ball that projects
beyond the bottom of the hoof. These snow balls make travel precarious.
Limited protection can be had by packing the clefts with Vaseline, oil-base
modeling clay, or some other moldable substance that is not water soluble.

Don't stress a horse when the temperature is below 10° Fahrenheit. Ice
crystals can form and damage the lungs when the horse draws in gasps of
air. Also, don't expect a horse to leap through powdery, chest-deep snow pulling a loaded sleigh. Shallow, hard-packed, or plowed surfaces are best for
sleighing. Since many horses do not get regular exercise in winter they tend
to be high-spirited when taken outside the barn. The excitement may cause
a joyful bucking or kicking spree. Brisk forward movement is the best prevention and cure. As a warm-up and muscle-stretching exercise, it is a good idea
to longe, if you have access to an indoor arena, or to walk the horse up and
down the barn aisle for several minutes before he is hooked. The driver must
be prepared with gloves that will keep the fingers warm, and allow a firm
grip on the reins.

One last caution: know the ground beneath the sleigh. This is essential, because snow can cover or camouflage hazards.

Whatever the rigors of winter, a sleigh ride along a peaceful country road between muffled rows of majestic pines can be an unparalleled treat for the pleasure driver. But enough said. The next chapter takes a look at the very different, high-pressure world of the breed ring.

6

THE BREED RING

The peacocks of driving are the harness horses who perform in the breed ring. They are preened, polished, and painstakingly trained to burst, with breathtaking presence, into the show arena and thrill stands of spectators, devoted railbirds, and exacting judges. The harness is minimal, without breeching or neck collar to obscure the view of a wonderful deep shoulder, level croup or long arched neck. It is elegant, too, sewn of butter-soft leather and decorated with elaborate strips of glossy black or colored

Ill. 6-1. The Morgan Park Horse. Stephen P. Davis driving UVM Heidi, a Morgan mare owned by the University of Vermont Morgan Horse Farm, and undefeated in 1982 in three-year-old park harness classes. (Photographer/Equus Studio)

patent leather and brass fittings. The vehicles are low and light, featuring two or four sparkling chrome wheels. The driver is the only passenger. These horses are not expected to work at pulling a load. Their energy is conserved for brilliant performance, be it a knee-popping collected trot or a spectacular extended trot. Breed-ring horses and their drivers are entertainers. For them, the whoops and yells of an excited audience are the background music for a drive in the limelight. Whether or not they win, they thrive on the proximity of blankets of roses, yokes of tricolored ribbon, and silver loving cups.

Breed-Ring Horses

Breed-ring horses are advertisements for their breed. They are the "cream of the crop," chosen for above-average conformation and ability. Only a small percentage of the registered members of a breed are trained to show in driving classes at American Horse Shows Association A-rated shows. They are special horses, representing a breeder's prize stock, a trainer's talent, or an amateur's best effort at the sport. As with all driving horses, basic care and harness training come first. But unlike the pleasure-driving horse of the previous chapter, who can fend for himself at intervals without losing his desirable traits and skills, the breed-ring horse needs diligent care and advanced training if he is going to meet the requirements of the show ring.

Several breeds routinely offer harness divisions at their private shows. For years there have been driving classes for Saddlebreds, Morgan Horses, and Arabians, and these have now become so specialized that horses within the breed cannot enter different categories. Appaloosa and Quarter Horse show committees, in tune with the suitability of these breeds for driving and with the increasing interest of competitors, are offering driving classes at large regional and year-end championship shows. Each of these groups specifies unique equipment and specialized performance for the horses. This chapter offers, first, general information on preparing a horse for the show ring, and a definition of the common breed-ring concept of "collection." It goes on to describe classes, equipment, and some training methods used to school several breeds of harness horses.

Special Care

The breed ring is a sophisticated and competitive environment. According to the rulebook, the horses are judged on performance, manners, and conformation, but cosmetic appearance plays an equally important part. For instance, an entrant in a crowded class has to arrest the attention of the judge. Obviously, a glistening coat, bright white markings, and a general appearance of health and good muscle tone are eye-catching. Also, an impeccably "turned-out" horse adds polish to a good performance. Two horses may execute class qualifications with equal skill and mannerly zest, but when pressed for a decision, the judge will choose the better-groomed horse. On a subtle level, show-ring etiquette dictates that exhibitors show respect for the judge. Many judges consider poor presentation a form of disrespect. Since much of breed-ring judging is subjective, based on personal preference, hours of preparation and money invested in equipment and show fees are wasted if the judge is insulted by an exhibitor's appearance. "Turn-out" is often the dividing line between the novice and the pro, yet it is the least difficult aspect of show preparation to master.

The foundation for a finished show-ring appearance is a year-round program combining sensible nutrition, exercise, and grooming. Commercial preparations applied to the horse's coat on the day of a show will not turn dull, shaggy hair into a show coat. The glow must come from within, so be prepared to begin developing coat condition months in advance of a show. Clipping, bathing, conditioners, and oils are only last-minute enhancers.

The show horse faces a demanding schedule. The stress of training and competing requires him to expend much more energy than is asked of a backyard pleasure-driving horse. Hay is an insufficient diet; the addition of grain to add starch (an easily utilized source of energy) to the diet is recommended. The amount of grain, as well as the ratio of hay to grain, depends upon the individual horse. Many trainers substitute a reliable pelleted feed for much of the hay. A small flake of hay is fed at midday to ease boredom and satisfy the instinctive equine need for stemmy forage. Pellets have two advantages over hay. First, the horseman can be sure of the quality of the feed. Poor or damaged hay, on the other hand, can be unavoidable, expensive, and debilitating to the condition of a show horse. Second, pellets don't produce "hay belly," the condition of a bloated abdomen caused by poor-quality hay passing slowly through the digestive tract. Pellets are often an all-inclusive feed, containing vitamins and minerals, whereas a diet of hay and grain requires the addition of a vitamin-mineral supplement. All horses require free-choice salt and access to fresh water.

The addition of corn oil to the feeding program can dramatically improve the condition of skin and hair. Corn oil contains essential fatty acids (linoleic, linolenic, and arachadonic) vital to maintenance of a healthy coat. Daily pour two tablespoons to ¼ cup over the grain ration. Carrots can be another important feed supplement. They contain natural vitamin A, which is important to healthy skin but difficult to store in commercially-prepared form. Commercially packaged coat conditioners are available in pelleted, powdered, and liquid form. These contain chemical counterparts of fatty acids plus some vitamins and minerals. Check the list of ingredients to be sure they are compatible with other supplements included in the feeding program. Strike a balance. Too much of a single vitamin or mineral can be counteractive, even harmful.

The emphasis on coat condition relegates the show horse to the status of a "hot house flower"; the only suitable housing for him is a private stall. The pasture presents too many natural hazards. Sunlight bleaches and dries the skin and hair. Nicks, bruises, and scrapes are unavoidable if there are other horses in the pasture or if it contains brush, trees, or rocky ground. Perfect footing is also essential for breed-ring horses that are equipped with weighted shoes. When these horses throw a shoe they usually lose a section of the hoof wall with it. Thus, a shoeing accident can put them out of service for weeks or months. The weighted shoes also alter the natural balance of the horse. Often the guidance of a handler is necessary to prevent interfering or overreaching at fast gaits. Take precautions if a show horse is allowed free time in a paddock. Be sure the ground is level and soft—but not deep—and free of mud, ice, and rocks. The fence should be smooth so that no projecting nail or sliver of wood can cause a disfigurement. Put the horse out at dusk or after dark (if lights are available), or protect the coat from the sun with a turn-out sheet. Put protective boots on all four legs if the horse is wearing weighted shoes.

Ultraviolet rays which damage coat condition are present on cloudy as well as sunny days. For optimum protection, plan training sessions for early morning or late afternoon hours. Work during the day inside a covered arena or in the shade. Don't leave the horse tied on a hot walker; hand walk him in the shade until he is cool.

Horses in warm southern climates are shown all year round. The rainy season, though relatively warm, triggers growth of a heavy coat. These horses must be "body clipped" in preparation for a show. The entire body of the horse is shaved. A heavy-duty clipper and special blade are necessary. Some horses are an unattractive color after they are body clipped; clipping these horses six weeks before the show will ensure enough growth to return the coat to its normal color. A body-clipped horse requires a special winter wardrobe. A heavy blanket and hood are necessary during the cold evening hours and a light blanket on cool days.

A long, full tail, which is prized by devotees of the breed ring, requires special attention. The tail may be kept braided or "tied up" to encourage growth and prevent the hairs from breaking. The tail hairs are carefully separated and picked clean of debris. This is usually done by hand, although gentle brushing is acceptable. The tail is then shampooed, rinsed until absolutely clean, and dried. A mane and tail conditioner is massaged into the hair. For braiding, you will need three strips of 1-inch-wide waterproof acetate ribbon (available in a wide range of colors at tack stores). Cut them several inches longer than the length of the tail and knot them together at one end. Hold the knotted end of ribbon against the hair on the underside of the tail, just below the tail bone. Separate the hair into three equal segments, holding a strand of ribbon with each segment. Braid the hair and ribbon tightly to the end of the tail. Tie the ends of the ribbon around the base of the braid to hold it together. Next, fold the end of the braid upward and thread it through the top of the braid, from the inside out, and back through the braid several inches

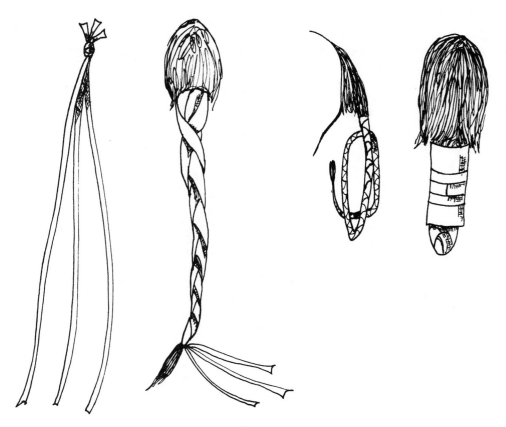

Ill. 6-2. Procedure for tying up a tail.

below this point, to form a knot. Wrap the ends of ribbon securely around the knot and tie them to hold the knot in place. Cut a rectangle of disposable cotton (leg wrap or a diaper with the plastic removed) the width of the knot. Wrap the cotton tightly around the knot and tape it in place with masking tape. During fly season you can provide some protection against insects by tying strips of ribbons to the base of the knot. This method of tying up a tail is efficient and longlasting. Don't leave the knot in place for more than two weeks, however, because urine can saturate the knot and rot the tail hair. Repeat the procedure of untying, washing, and rebraiding.

A refined throttle is necessary for comfortable poll flexion. Fitting a horse with a jowl sweat (felt in the stall and Neoprene during workouts) helps with horses that have thick throttles. A jowl sweat causes the neck to sweat, thus cells beneath it become dehydrated, i.e., lose water. A sweat also flattens the hair. The effect is temporary, but a horse's jowl is slimmer when a sweat is used consistently.

Some special care is necessary on the day before and the day of the show. The horse is show-clipped. A hand-held clipper with a fine-toothed blade is used to remove hair and whiskers. The bridle path, the portion of the mane directly behind the ears, is shaved close. The width of the bridle path depends on the breed. Saddlebreds, Morgans, and Arabians have 6- to 10-inch bridle paths to accentuate the length of the neck and the fineness of the throttle. Narrow bridle paths, just wide enough to accommodate the crownpiece of the bridle, are customary with other breeds. The hair inside and around the edges of the ears is removed. Many horses resent this process; it may be necessary to have assistance. In fact, it is a good idea to find out before purchase whether a potential show horse tolerates this procedure. Otherwise you may have to call on a veterinarian to tranquilize the horse before every show so that its ears can be clipped. All the whiskers on the face should be removed as well as the long hair beneath the chin and jawbones. The hair around the fetlocks and coronet bands also is clipped, and white socks are shaved.

Apply Vaseline to the chestnuts on the inside of the legs; in a few hours they will be soft and can be peeled away. Ergots, tiny claws that project from the back of the fetlocks, should be trimmed close to the joint.

The horse is bathed to remove clipped hair, dandruff, dust, dirt, and stains from the coat; use a shampoo formulated for horses. If the horse is white or light in color, special shampoos containing bleach and brighteners are available. Rinse the soap from the coat. Apply a conditioner to the mane and tail. Rinse. If the tail is dragging on the ground, loop it in a simple temporary knot to prevent the horse from standing on it and tearing out the hair. Lay a cooler or skim sheet over the horse to keep dust from settling on the coat while he is drying. When it is too cold to bathe the horse, use a stable vacuum to clean the coat. A brisk currying will raise dirt to the surface and the vacuum will suck it away. Commercial preparations sold at tack stores and called dry cleaners can be used to remove stains from the coat. Cover the horse with a fly sheet, day sheet, or blanket (depending on the temperature of the day) before returning him to the stall. (A clean horse will roll the instant an opportunity presents itself.)

On the day of the show, after the regular grooming, apply a liquid or spray dressing to the coat. Hand-rub or towel the hair to a high sheen, then cover the horse with a skim sheet or cooler until the class is called, otherwise the coat dressing will attract dust. Apply cornstarch or talc liberally to white socks to achieve a stark whiteness. Take down the tail and gently brush it out. Tie the tail in a simple, temporary knot until it is time for the class.

Prepare the hooves by removing any shavings, straw, or manure, that may be packed in the frog cleft. Scrub the hoof wall clean. Some competitors, thirsting for perfection, use a fine sand paper and grind the hoof wall smooth (most farriers don't approve of this practice because it weakens the hoof wall). Apply a coating of matching hoof color, covering each hoof. Take care not to let the color bleed onto white socks. Use tape as a guide when coloring striped hoofs. When the first application is dry apply a coat of clear polish for additional shine. Some exhibitors add a polyurethane coating over the hoof color. This makes the hoof glow like patent leather, but the coating seals the porous structure and must be sanded away after the show, destroying still more of the hoof wall.

As a final touch before entering the show ring, the eyes of the horse can be enhanced by coating the surrounding hair with mineral oil. If the skin eventually flakes and cracks in response to the product—as happens with some individuals—Vaseline can be substituted. In addition, some horse owners apply mascara to the lashes and/or darken the surrounding hair with eye shadow to make the eyes appear large and soulful. Be sure all orifices are clean. The inner ears, nostrils, and muzzle also benefit from a coat of oil. However, take care not to let the mineral oil drip down into the ear. Apply the oil sparingly to an absorbent cloth or cotton and transfer it to the ear.

A show horse spends a lot of time in a van or trailer traveling to and from shows. Prepare the horse for a comfortable, safe ride. Protect the lower legs, coronet bands, and heels with protective boots. A helmet, to protect the poll, should be attached to the halter. Use a trailer tie equipped with a quick-release snap. Be sure the ramp leading into the trailer and the flooring in the stall are not slippery. Don't feed coarse pellets, grain, or chunks of carrots or apples after the horse is tied. The short tie necessary for safe travel makes it impossible for the horse to stretch his neck and cough, which he might need to do to dislodge an obstruction. Hay is suitable feed to keep the animal busy during the ride. Allow adequate ventilation, but keep the horse dry and warm. Blanket him as the weather dictates. A closed trailer and a heavy blanket on a warm day will result in a sweaty, unhappy horse on arrival at the show grounds. After unloading, allow the horse to sip water, then walk for a few minutes before removing the leg wraps.

Special Training

All show horses benefit from a thorough, relaxed schedule of basic training (such as the one described in chapter 3), but there the similarity ends. The advanced training that prepares these horses for specialized performance in harness classes is unique to each breed as well as to specialists within each breed. For instance, a pleasure-driving Morgan and a park harness Morgan are equipped and schooled with different emphases to fulfill individual class qualifications. However, one goal—elegant balance, or "collection"—is sought after by all trainers of breed-ring harness horses, regardless of type.

When a horse is moving naturally, most of his weight is in front of an imaginary central line that bisects the body behind the forequarters. A relaxed horse that is moving freely, without interference, travels "on the forehand" or, as G. F. Corley describes this type of balance in his book, *Riding and Schooling the Western Performance Horse*, with "forward balance." The head and neck are extended in front of the body and carried low. The body of the horse is elongated. He moves economically from the shoulder and hips with a minimum of knee and hock action. There is potential for engagement and thus great drive from the hindquarters, permitting fast forward speeds. A race horse is forward balanced.

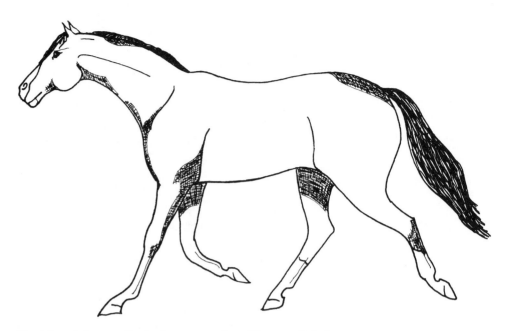

Ill. 6-3. A horse displaying natural or "forward" balance.

The collected movements and slow forward speeds of the show-ring horse are not natural. Seldom does a horse feel compelled to expend the energy required to perform these short, elevated steps. A startled horse may collect momentarily, but he quickly forsakes this state of balance for the comfort and speed of naturally balanced movement. The ability to collect and maintain collection must be learned. Months of patient, knowledgeable schooling are required to teach the horse to redistribute his weight and to develop the muscling necessary for holding the position. Extreme collection, displayed by dressage horses, results from years of training.

The profile of the collected horse is radically different from that of a horse displaying forward balance. The collected horse appears tall due to the elevation of the neck, and shorter from nose to tail because the head is flexed at the poll and the nose is drawn inward toward the chest (the face line will be vertical or almost vertical to the ground). The elevation of the neck and head shift the weight rearward, and the shift is further accentuated by engaged hindquarters (the haunches are lowered and the legs are well under the body). The rearward weight shift, coupled with a raised neck and upright head carriage allow for more knee and hock action. When a horse is collected, forward movement becomes high, round, and airy, never long-strided or ground-covering.

Collection differs in appearance depending on the conformation of the horse. In the Morgan, the neck is set more above than in front of the shoulder; an elevated head and neck are natural. The neck set of the Quarter Horse is in front of the withers. It is relatively easy, with the aid of traditional driving equipment, to hold the Morgan's neck up and his head close to the body;

Ill. 6-4. A collected dressage horse. (Artwork/Susan Carter)

this is termed "head set." But unless the hindquarters are engaged and the hocks elevated, collection is not present. In other words, a head set is necessary to collection, but a horse's head can be set without achieving collection. The Quarter Horse will not attain the elevation common to the Morgan and Saddlebred, but it can learn collection. When spinning, for example, a stock horse is collected. It is important to recognize all the points of collection. It is a state of balance that predisposes the horse to move in a certain way. Artificial aids can strap the horse into a position that gives the fleeting impression of collection, but true collection is only attained with painstaking schooling that teaches a horse (regardless of breed conformation) to redistribute his weight and maintain impulsion.

Work in harness has many advantages when teaching a horse to collect. Many upper-level dressage trainers in Europe do much of their schooling for collection during sessions of ground-driving and long-lining. It is easier for the horse to lighten his forehand if he doesn't have the added weight of a rider bearing down on his forequarters. Also, harness equipment can be used as an aid (though it should never be used as an artificial support) to teach the

Ill. 6-5.   A tight bearing rein and a short martingale can impede collection.

horse the new position. The checkrein will raise his head, although this must be done slowly, a hole at a time, over a number of training periods. If the checkrein is short, hook it when the horse is moving forward and unhook it when the animal is expected to stand for any period of time. It should never be so short that it interferes with normal flexion at the poll. This is self-defeating. A martingale can be used to give leverage on the bit (breed-ring horses traditionally are trained and usually shown in snaffles; never use a martingale with a curb bit). The increased leverage encourages the horse to flex at the poll and bring his nose inward. Again, the martingale must not be too short. If so, it will pull the horse's head and neck down. The martingale should not pull the reins into a downward angle between the bit and the ring terret on the saddle.

The position of the trainer, behind the horse, encourages engagement of the hindquarters and vigorous forward impulsion. The horse is convinced to move onto the bit and then is held together with the aid of the bit. In other words, strong forward impulsion in response to voice and whip (a touch of the lash on the side or belly will cause the croup to lower and draw the rear legs under the body) is redirected and transferred into up-and-down motion.

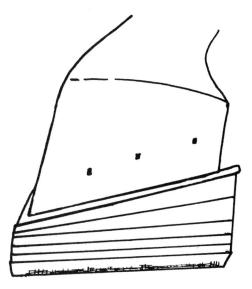

Ill. 6-6. A padded shoe.

A strong contact is necessary, but pulling will encourage a horse to push against the bit and brace his neck, which is the antithesis of the desired flexed poll and soft jaw. Once the horse has learned to collect and is physically prepared for the task he will be light-mouthed, provided you have worked to achieve this from early training onward. During fleeting first moments of successful performance, as well as later in training, reward his mouth with a sensitive supportive contact. Don't drop or throw the horse away. For many months he will be dependent upon the driver to define the boundaries of this new balance.

Additional aids may be used by breed-ring trainers to teach their horses the mechanics of collected movement. Long toes, weighted shoes, pads, and/or chains and rattlers are used to encourage the horses to move from the knees and hocks. Much of the high action displayed by breed-ring horses is the result of the increased energy needed to break over an abnormally long toe while lifting an abnormally heavy hoof off the ground. Horses who are limited as to the amount of weight they can carry on their hooves in the show ring often are trained with rattlers and chains buckled around the pasterns. The sound, and weight of these annoying bracelets encourages short, elevated strides. Another device, training shackles, is used to strengthen the muscles of the forequarters, thus improving the potential for high action. Shackles are a form of isometric exercise whereby the horse pulls against elastic straps during movement.

Every breed-ring trainer has secrets of the trade, but one method seems common and effective if preliminary work has taught the horse to flex at the poll, engage his hindquarters, and move forward from a cluck. A plastic bag or popper is tied to the thong of a longe whip. During a long-lining session an assistant moves to a point in front of the horse, halfway around the training circle. He softly shakes the modified whip in the animal's path (whip movement can become more vigorous once the horse is accustomed to the procedure). The assistant backs off instantly after the diversion; he must never be so close to the horse that he is perceived as a real threat. The horse, upon seeing the whip, will elevate his neck, tuck his head, shorten his body, and perhaps momentarily trot in place. In essence, the horse collects. The trainer now must insist on forward impulsion. The horse should be disciplined if he breaks gait, comes off his feet, or attempts to spin. Keep these sessions brief or the horse will become bored and unresponsive. Never frighten the horse. If properly used, these interludes are an enjoyable and instructive game that teaches collected animation. Once the horse is steady, understands what is going to happen, and maintains forward movement, the procedure can be used when he is hooked to the cart.

The Morgan

The Morgan Horse, since the inception of the breed, has been prized for his ability to perform in harness. During the 1800s, Morgans proved their versatility. A horse might work at skidding logs and plowing fields, provide stylish transportation when hooked to the family wagon for a trip into town, and then compete in a trotting race for the entertainment of its owner. Contemporary Morgans continue to be coveted for their versatility and skill in harness. This is reflected in the number and variety of well-filled driving classes at Morgan breed shows. They are shown in park harness, pleasure-driving, antique carriage, and roadster classes and compete in harness races at private breed shows.

Morgans are ideally suited for driving because of their characteristic attitude and conformation. They are noted for a muscular, compact body and level croup. The neck is set above the withers and supported by an extremely long, sloping, and deep shoulder. The typical Morgan head is expressive, featuring a broad forehead and large, liquid eye. The softness of the eye is reflected in a tractable disposition. Gentle willingness combines with spirit and stamina. These traits make Morgans ideal harness horses for the show ring as well as for other harness sports.

Park Harness

The park harness Morgan is a spectacular, stylish harness horse and represents breed excellence for many Morgan fanciers. He performs boldly in harness, displaying high, round action and a regal demeanor. With neck elevated, head vertical, croup lowered, and hindquarters engaged, he has the lightness and impulsion necessary to move around the show arena with brilliant and animated elegance. A good park horse is never coarse in conformation or labored in his movements. He must be balanced and graceful both in appearance and "way of going."

Equipment for park harness classes enhances the natural beauty of the horse. A "fine" breast-collar harness, constructed of narrow leather and rolled where applicable (traces and reins), is recommended. The harness is black with brass fittings. Blinders, saddle, and breast collar are decorated with black patent leather. The cavesson and brow band may display a colored patent leather stripe. The reins are always brown and often equipped with stitched leather loops called "hand holds."

Park Morgans are generally shown wearing a snaffle bit and a check bit hooked to an overcheck or sidecheck bearing rein. A martingale is used with a snaffle. A liverpool bit, in combination with a check bit and sidecheck bearing rein, is also acceptable.

A low, light, four-wheeled, rubber-tired viceroy (also called a sidebar fine harness wagon) is the vehicle used in park harness classes. The body is painted a deep subtle color and pin-striped. The wheel rims and spokes and any additional hardware items are of chrome.

Regulations allow the park Morgan a maximum toe length of 5 3/4 inches, including shoe and pad. There is no limit on shoe weight. The length of the toe of the first-place winner of championship and stakes classes is measured before the horse is allowed to leave the ring.

One passenger, the driver, is allowed in the cart. He or she should be neatly attired in a conservative suit or jacket and trousers, narrow brimmed fedora-type hat, or a small feminine hat, sturdy shoes or boots, and gloves. Women often wear dresses. A whip is optional according to the rules, but a whip in hand gives a more professional appearance to the turnout. One attendant is allowed to enter the ring and "head up" the horse during the lineup. The attendant may uncheck the horse, assist in standing the animal in the traditional parked position, and quickly wipe off the muzzle and bit—unless the judge is approaching to inspect the horse. When the judge is in attendance the attendant must stand quietly to one side of the head, never blocking the view of the horse. Attendants, like other persons in the show arena, should be neatly attired. Jacket, trousers, boots, and gloves make an acceptable outfit. An attendant may carry a towel.

The park horse is judged on performance, presence, quality, manners, type, and conformation. He must be a majestic and stylish harness horse as he executes the required gaits—an animated walk and an animated trot. The animated walk is not flat-footed. It is an airy, aristocratic, alert, four-beat collected gait. The animated trot is a two-beat collected gait. The horse should exhibit extreme, balanced elevation of knees and hocks while "moving on," but without excessive speed. Speed results in a loss of collection and is penalized. Counterflexing (bending the head and neck to one side), pacing, winging, and paddling are considered faults. A park horse should be "up in the bridle" (alert, collected), and on the bit but never pulling against the driver or coming behind contact.

No amount of training can transform a poorly conformed, lackadaisical Morgan into a park horse. He must be born with athletic ability and a show-horse attitude. Given these natural ingredients, the trainer teaches basic harness skills, then proceeds to train the horse to perform collected gaits. Brief moments of animated collection are gradually lengthened as the horse gains stamina. Short training sessions are best. The horse should be fresh and up for his work. High spirits are channeled into zestful performance. Weighted shoes are necessary to achieve the height of action required by today's competitive show atmosphere.

The park horse must also learn to assume the specialized "parked" stance common in the line-up. This skill can be taught early and reinforced during preliminary training. Back the horse until his hind feet are square and then ask him to come forward without moving those feet. It may be necessary to move the front legs mechanically. Touching the front legs with a whip encourages their movement. Repeat the command (*Park, Stretch, On your feet,* or *Stand up*) as the legs are positioned. Command *Ho* if the horse moves a leg and repositions it. When correctly parked, the hind legs of the horse are stretched behind the haunches, the croup is level, and the front legs are ver-

Ill. 6-7.   The "park" stance.

tical. The body of the horse is rocked forward over the front legs. The neck is elevated and the head flexed at the poll. Bait the horse with a treat when teaching him to move forward over the front legs and raise his neck. Overstretching causes the back to sag and gives the appearance of poor conformation. After several training sessions the horse will move into the stance, on command, without assistance.

Pleasure Driving

The Morgan in pleasure-driving classes is expected to have good breed conformation, a spirited show-ring attitude, less action than a park horse, and a steadier approach to performance of the gaits. This horse is judged on his ability to perform pleasurably in harness as well as on manners, gaits, type, and conformation. The pleasure-driving horse is expected to walk, pleasure trot, and road trot.

The correct harness for pleasure driving is slightly more substantial than harness for park classes. It calls for a black "dressy" breast collar, a colorful cavesson set, brass fittings, and black patent leather decorations. The leather of the show harness can be sewn round as it is for park harness. Pleasure-driv-

Ill. 6-8. A Morgan pleasure-driving horse. Ann Knoll driving Knollcrest Bit O' Magic.

ing horses are always shown in traditional half-cheek snaffles, check bits, and overcheck or sidecheck bearing reins. A martingale is part of the equipment.

A two-wheeled show cart or a four-wheeled viceroy is an acceptable vehicle, although a two-wheeled cart is considered more appropriate. A show cart is a variation of a jog cart. It has wooden shafts attached to a tubular metal undercarriage and two rubber-tired chrome wheels bolted to the metal frame. The seat is set on a block above a two- or three-leafed system of springs. A wooden basket screws to the frame and serves as a footrest. The basket is covered with a vinyl boot that snaps in place and gives a neat appearance. A small dash protects the driver from flying mud or dirt. The wood and metal is painted and pin-striped.

Shoeing regulations for pleasure Morgans limit toe length to 4-3/4-inches including shoes and pads, and shoe weight to 18 ounces, including pads. Most farriers agree that a pleasure Morgan is most effectively and comfortably shod with a long toe coupled with a wedge pad and a shoe of evenly distributed weight.

One passenger—the driver—is allowed in the vehicle. He or she should be dressed in either a contemporary country casual or a businesslike style. This includes a jacket, small hat, sturdy shoes, and gloves. A saddle suit is also correct. A whip, though not required, is more professional looking. One neatly attired attendant can stand at the head of the horse during the lineup. An attendant should not fuss with a pleasure-driving horse, especially in ladies' or junior classes. A horse qualified for these classes must be mannerly.

The walk of the pleasure-driving horse is brisk though relaxed and flat-footed. He should be on the bit, flexed, and collected, but lacking the aggressive demeanor of the park horse. A pleasure-driving horse would be suitable for a low-key country drive, not for Sunday afternoon in Central Park. However, don't let the horse drag. He should appear willing, eager, and responsive to the driver at all gaits. The pleasure trot is a collected two-beat gait. The horse must perform with balance, style, and reasonable round action. A pleasure horse has to give the impression that he can travel a distance without fatigue. High park action would be inappropriate and should be penalized. The road trot is an extended gait. The horse must revert to semicollected balance. He must lower his head and neck and forsake some height of action for a longer stride. The gait should be ground-covering, though not excessively fast, and the horse should remain balanced and light on the bit.

Basic harness training, outlined in chapter 3, is good preparation for a pleasure-driving class and can be followed with schooling for collected balance at the walk and pleasure trot. Chains or rattlers may be used to encourage knee and hock action. The road trot requires some special training. It is not a natural gait and cannot be achieved by urging the horse to trot faster and faster. A track or a long, untraveled dirt road is the best training ground. Begin with a pleasure trot and slowly allow the horse more freedom of the head and neck while asking for increased impulsion. It is a good idea to choose a unique sound (for instance, a kiss) to signal this trot. The driver must support the horse at this gait. If the horse is heavy on the forehand, move the bit in his mouth, and touch him with the whip to engage the hindquarters. If he breaks, command *Trot* and hold the bit until he resumes the requested gait. Work slowly to build length of stride and stamina as well as the muscling and balance necessary for the horse to retain form at this most popular and critical pleasure gait (many pleasure classes are pinned on the quality of the road trot).

Large Morgan shows often offer other types of harness classes. There is always a roadster division. Equipment and training for roadsters of all breeds are discussed in the last section of this chapter. Antique-carriage classes are becoming increasingly popular. Class specifications and equipment are determined by American Driving Society rules. Information about showing in this category is covered in chapter 7. Americana classes are included at some shows in some locales. These are antique-carriage classes in which the driver and passengers dress in period costume. One other class, the Justin Morgan, is a true test of Morgan versatility. Competitors trot a half-mile in harness, gallop a half-mile under saddle, perform a walk, trot, and canter in the show ring, and pull a stone boat (weighing a minimum of 500 pounds) for a distance of 6 feet. Each section accounts for 25 percent of the points, but a horse who fails to pull the stone boat the required distance is eliminated.

The Saddlebred

The Saddlebred is a born and bred aristocrat. Early breeders needed a distinct type of horse to provide stylish, smooth-gaited, and mannerly transportation—under saddle and in harness—for plantation owners and their families during the nineteenth century. These breeders, concentrated in Virginia, North and South Carolina, and Kentucky, acquired outstanding representatives of the Morgan and Standardbred as well as lesser-known breeds, and crossbred their offspring to get a unique set of talents. The result was the characteristic Saddlebred.

The Saddlebred is an eye-catching, noble horse. He has an attractive head remarkable for its broad forehead, wide, intelligent eyes, and refined throttle. The head is set on a long, curving neck above well-defined withers. He has a deep, sloping shoulder that accounts for natural, free, elevated movement. The body is close-coupled, the croup level, and the tail set high. Muscular quarters, straight legs, and long, sloping pasterns are the basis for the smooth and comfortable gaits prized by southern ladies. The elegant proportions, lofty action, and bright but tractable disposition, make the Saddlebred a regal showring harness horse.

Saddlebred breed shows sponsor two major harness divisions: fine harness

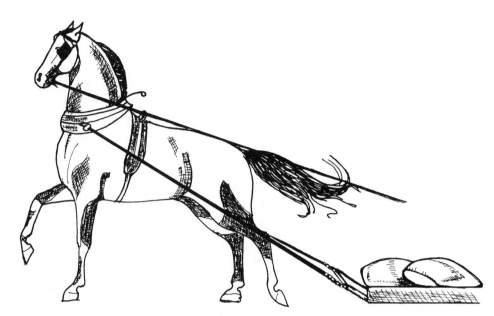

Ill. 6-9. A Morgan pulling a stone boat, one of four sections of the Justin Morgan class.

and pleasure driving. Most shows also offer roadster classes (information about roadsters is included in the last section of this chapter). Three-gaited horses are provided with a combination class. They are shown in harness and under saddle and judged equally on each skill. A fine harness and a four-wheeled viceroy or sidebar fine harness wagon are correct equipment for this class. The mane of a three-gaited Saddlebred is roached and the tail set. (A veterinarian surgically alters the tail carriage of a horse when it is young. After this is done, the horse wears a tail brace when not working. The result of the surgery and the brace is high tail carriage.) Country pleasure is a variation on pleasure driving, but the horse must be flat shod (no pads) and have a natural mane and tail (tails that were once set are allowed though the horse will no longer wear a brace and retains some of the characteristics of a surgically-altered tail). A country pleasure horse cannot be shown with ribboned braids or additional hair on the tail.

Fine Harness

The fine-harness Saddlebred stands paramount among the members of his breed. He exhibits great strength and brilliance when performing the required gaits. Breeders compete avidly for championship titles in this division, and fine-harness champions are coveted breeding stock.

A black, breast-collar harness is correct for a fine-harness class. It must be constructed of high-quality leather and be decorated with patent leather

Ill. 6-10. A "fine-harness" Saddlebred.

and brass fittings. The traces and reins usually are sewn round or "rolled." The crupper may have a raised brace to hold the tail high and an attachment for a false tail. A snaffle and check bit, an overcheck bearing rein, and a running martingale are standard equipment. A four-wheeled viceroy or sidebar fine harness wagon is the proper vehicle. The overall impression is one of unencumbered elegance.

The fine-harness horse is shown with a full mane and tail which may be given the appearance of abundance with inconspicuously applied additional hair. Long toes, weighted shoes, and stacked pads are customary and necessary to attain spectacularly high action. Quarter boots are worn on the front hooves and colorful ribbon is braided into the first section of the mane. The white boots highlight the grand elevation of the front legs, the ribbons add a touch of frivolous gaiety, and the addition of false hair rounds out the flowing symmetry, creating a majestic picture.

The driver is the only passenger. He or she should wear a conservative riding suit. Hat, gloves, and whip are customary. An attendant is allowed to enter the ring for the lineup or stand inside the ring during ladies', junior, and amateur classes. The attendant should be neatly attired.

Fine-harness horses perform a walk and park trot. A third gait, termed "show your horses," is requested in open classes. Entries are judged on quality, performance, and manners. The walk is animated and collected; the horse springs with graceful ease as he executes each stride. The trot is also collected, featuring high, round, spectacularly balanced action. Winging, interfering, traveling wide, counterflexing, paddling, and excessive speed are penalized. The horse should move airily and gracefully forward, exhibiting strength and endurance that are the result of a prepossessing confident attitude and a sound muscular physique. At the command *Show your horse*, the exhibitors ask their horse to perform a trot that demonstrates the peak of their ability. The aim is not speed, but a magnification of the best features of the park trot.

Training of fine-harness horses follows the same general procedures used to develop Morgan park horses. Animated collected gaits are encouraged as the checkrein is gradually shortened to achieve optimum neck elevation. Soft poll flexion and a relaxed jaw are essential to keep this bold, bridled horse manageable. Hindquarter engagement supplies the impulsion necessary for unhampered forequarters. The Saddlebred "parks" in the lineup.

Pleasure Driving

Much the same is expected of a pleasure-driving Saddlebred (Ill. 1–10) as from a pleasure-driving Morgan. A mannerly attitude should replace the volatile presence necessary to a fine-harness horse. Nonetheless, dullness is always out of place in the show ring. The performance should contain elements of willing spirit and bright personality. A pleasure-driving horse can be equipped with weighted shoes and pads, braids, and additional hair, but not with quarter boots. This horse must be driven by an amateur or by a junior exhibitor.

The same equipment used for pleasure driving Morgans is correct for their Saddlebred counterparts.

Drivers generally wear saddle suits, a derby hat, and gloves and carry whip in hand. Gentlemen drivers wear a fedora-type hat.

Training outlined for the pleasure Morgans will prepare the Saddlebred for a driving class. The road trot is termed an "extended trot," though the specifications are the same. These horses are required to park in the lineup, stand quietly, and back readily. (See chapter 5 for information on training a driving horse to back.) Manners, quality, and performance are judged during a Saddlebred pleasure-driving class.

The Arabian

The Arabian is a classic horse. A fine, dished face, large, prominent eyes, long, slender, arched neck, finely modeled body and legs, are accented by a high tail carriage. This combination gives the Arabian the impression of unrivaled equine beauty. The minimal equipment customary for breed-ring driving serves to enhance the esthetically pleasing conformation while harness skills offer a proving ground for testing the well-known "heart" and intelligence of this exceptional breed. Arabians are shown in three divisions: formal driving, pleasure driving, and roadster classes. Formal driving bears some resemblance to park or fine harness, as does pleasure driving to the pleasure-driving divisions of the two previous breeds. But there are important differences devised to protect the natural beauty of the Arabian.

The equipment for formal driving is the same as for park harness, except that a curb bit is never acceptable. Pleasure-driving harness is also common for the three breeds, but although two-wheeled show carts are permitted according to the rules, viceroys or sidebar fine harness wagons are the most usual vehicles in these classes.

The driver is the only passenger allowed in either division. A saddle suit is traditional attire. Attendants are allowed to head Arabians during the line-up; they must be neatly dressed.

Shoeing regulations are rigid. Maximum length of toe is 4 1/2-inches,

Ill. 6-11. An Arabian "formal driving" horse. (Artwork/Susan Carter)

Ill. 6-12. An Arabian pleasure-driving horse. (Artwork/Susan Carter)

and maximum shoe weight (excluding nails) is 12 ounces.

The Arabian is expected to move from the shoulder with free, floating action. The hindquarters are engaged, positioned well under the body, and the hocks are active. This horse must show no sign of laboring or pounding. The intensity of the performance is derived from its fluidity and precision, although the Arabian in formal-driving classes must give a confident performance and display a bold "fire-eating" attitude. Manners, quality, and performance are judged.

Training for formal- and pleasure-driving Arabians can closely parallel that for the companion divisions of the previous breeds, keeping the above information in mind. Different terms are used in requesting the gaits although their performance (aside from style of action) is the same. Formal-driving horses perform a brisk collected walk and an animated collected trot. Pleasure horses are asked to execute a collected, flat-footed walk, a normal trot, and a strong trot.

The Quarter Horse

The speedy, strong, and enduring Quarter Horse makes an excellent, though radically different, harness horse from the three previously mentioned breeds. He is a down-to-earth performer, and frills are as alien to his style as is elevated action. The Quarter Horse is noted for his easy disposition and steady, energy-conserving approach to performance. Although this breed is having exciting success in other areas of harness sport, especially combined driving, pleasure driving is the only harness division offered at breed shows.

Ill. 6-13. A pleasure-driving Quarter Horse.

This suggests that greater emphasis will be given to driving Quarter Horses in the future.

Pleasure-driving Quarter Horses wear a show harness like the one used for the pleasure-driving Morgan. It is generally a black breast-collar harness decorated with some patent leather and brass fittings. A neck collar and/or breeching are permitted but are not commonly used. The bit can be a snaffle used in conjunction with an overcheck bit, overcheck bearing rein, and martingale; or a curb bit, check bit, and sidecheck bearing rein. The curb chain must be flat and at least 1/2-inch wide. The usual vehicle is a two-wheeled show cart (described for the pleasure Morgan). The wheel diameter may range from 24 to 48 inches. A basket is always required but a boot is optional.

Quarter Horses are shown with natural hooves and standard shoes. Weights, stacked pads, and long toes are prohibited.

The driver is the only passenger allowed in the cart during the class. Neat attire, consisting of jacket and pants, hat, gloves, and whip, is customary. Skirts must be covered with a driving apron (Ill. 4–4). Attendants should not be necessary during the lineup.

Horses are judged on their suitability, skill, and conformation as it applies to driving. They are expected to walk, park gait (normal trot), and road gait (extended trot). They must back readily and stand quietly. The walk is flat-footed and forward-moving, never animated. The trot is an easy, efficient, two-beat gait. It should be effortless, square, and straight. The road gait must be ground-covering without loss of balance or excessive speed. Animation, action, and speed are penalized throughout the performance.

Basic harness training is a good beginning for the Quarter Horse. However, because steady performance and manners are paramount to a spirited performance, some exposure to instill confidence is necessary. Cross-country pleasure drives, besides providing an introduction to the world beyond the barn and ring, heighten the condition and endurance necessary to fulfill class qualification within the bounds of plebeian style. Also, you must know your horse. A horse show is an extraordinary experience, and the same preparation that gets a park or fine-harness horse "up" for his performance may put the pleasure-driving horse "on edge." If necessary, work him down. A few minutes driving in the warm-up area or around the grounds may make the difference in attitude during the class.

If the horse is to be shown "Texas-style," natural forward (though never strung-out) balance should be maintained. A "California-style" Quarter Horse must learn to perform with semicollected balance. Semicollection requires some neck elevation, a flexed poll, the nose 2 or 3 inches in front of the vertical line, engaged hindquarters, and a lowered croup. Semicollection is achieved in the same manner as collection, although extreme neck elevation, shortening of the body, and high action are not desired. Semicollection is the halfway point between forward balance and collection.

The Appaloosa

The Appaloosa combines symmetrical conformation and a varied but always colorful coat with a crafty, intelligent disposition and the strength and endurance to excel in harness. Like the Quarter Horse, the Appaloosa is expected to drive with decorum in the show ring. Vivid coat patterns aside, this horse must not appear to be a prima donna; he is expected to be industrious and singleminded about the performance of class qualifications. The horses are judged on suitability, skill, and conformation. They are requested to do a flat-footed walk, a normal trot, and a fast trot, to back, and to stand quietly without a header. Two divisions are offered to Appaloosa exhibitors at breed shows: pleasure driving and buckboard pleasure. Buckboard pleasure is essentially an antique-carriage class, although the vehicle must portray an early American or frontier-type of vehicle. The harness should be in keeping with the style of vehicle. Heavy vehicles require a sturdy, working neck-collar harness and a breeching. Period costumes, matched to the era of the bug-

Ill. 6-14. An Appaloosa turned out for a buckboard pleasure-driving class.

gy or wagon, are correct and are allotted 10 percent of the judge's total consideration.

The equipment for an Appaloosa pleasure-driving class is the same as for Quarter Horse pleasure driving, except that a four-wheeled vehicle is acceptable. The usual four-wheeled vehicle is a viceroy or sidebar fine-harness show cart. The driver (no pets) is the only passenger allowed in the vehicle. He or she should be neatly attired in the standard clothing previously described for pleasure driving. A lap robe or driving apron is necessary if the exhibitor is wearing a skirt. An attendant should not be required to hold the horse during the lineup.

Toe length and shoe weight are conservatively regulated. The Appaloosa cannot be shown with a toe exceeding 4 1/2-inches; the shoe must not weigh more than 14 ounces or be wider than 1 1/8-inches.

The Appaloosa and the Quarter Horse can be prepared for the breed ring following the same procedures as described earlier for the other breeds.

The Roadster

White quarter boots flash as the front legs of the roadster move with dizzying speed, and the hocks and hindquarters drive with power and precision. The driver balances on the edge of the seat and aims deep into the fast-approaching corners as the road horse burns up the ring. Spectators, who were sitting sedately in the stands just moments before, are on their feet roaring encouragement to these charismatic horses and their drivers. Roadster classes are the most crowd-pleasing harness classes common to the breed ring.

The roadster is a type, not a breed, of horse. Morgan, Saddlebred, and Arabian breed shows offer private classes, but large all-breed shows offer open roadster divisions in which members of these breeds, plus Standardbreds and crossbreds, compete.

Ill. 6-15. A road horse to bike. Edwin Freeman driving Miss Dean Key, seven times World Champion in this division. (Photographer/Sargent)

Roadster harness is very fine and lightweight, featuring a minimum of leather and fittings and weighing less than 15 pounds. It is black breast-collar harness (except roadster pairs who wear neck collars), and is equipped with leather cups, or "thimbles," that fit over the ends of the shafts and serve as breaks for lightweight vehicles. A snaffle bit, check bit, overcheck bearing rein, and martingale are customary. Breeching, rather than thimbles, is required in wagon classes.

Road horses are shown to two different types of vehicles: a bike or a wagon. The bike is a racing sulky. It is a light (less than 50 pounds), two-wheeled cart equipped with a single seat and stirrups. A road wagon is a four-wheeled vehicle with wooden wheels, usually featuring a hood and an under-carriage and body similiar to a sidebar fine-harness wagon. The hood is folded during classes.

For appointment classes, the roadster is shown to a road wagon. A set of equipment more extensive than a marathon spares kit must be carried in the wagon during circuits of the show ring. These items include: clock mounted on the dash, hoof pick, wheel wrench, blanket pins, wire pliers, horseshoes and nails, goggles, hammer, whisk, nail pliers, rasp, leather punch, sweat scraper, road blanket, lap robe, waterproof cover, tie strap, bandages, brush, halter, rub rags, overcoat, and dark-colored hat.

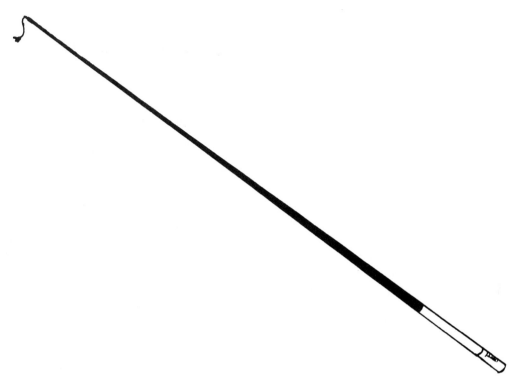

Ill. 6-16. A black whip with a short lash, white leather handle, and chrome cap. This type is commonly used in the breed ring.

The driver in bike classes wears a matching hat and jacket of colorful stable silks. The driver of a road wagon must wear a businesslike suit and a narrow brimmed hat. Gloves, goggles, and whip are customary additional equipment. Headers are not allowed in the ring.

Shoeing is generally not used to enhance performance of a roadster, at least not to the extent it is for park and fine-harness horses. The road horse is expected to possess innate trotting ability. Simple, light shoes are most common. White quarter boots are worn to protect the bulbs of the front hooves and add visual illusion to the trot.

Elementary harness training provides a foundation for the road horse, but much advanced training is necessary for a successful performance. He is expected to jog, road gait (fast trot), and trot on (full speed at the trot) in the narrow confines of the show ring. The horse is judged on performance, speed, quality, manners, and style. The roadster is expected to retain form or balance at all gaits. He must be semicollected, with neck elevated, head flexed at the poll, and legs well under the body. The horse must be on the bit, as illustrated by the phrase common to roadster buffs, "going with a set chin," but he must not be unresponsive. Even at speed, a road horse must be sensitive to bit pressure for the safety of all involved.

Balance is the basis of roadster training. Start at the jog trot and stay at that speed until the horse performs with his head, neck and body straight, while performing a squarely balanced trot, and can execute faultless serpentines, figure eights, and small circles. Stamina for speed can be developed outside a ring on a track or untraveled dirt road during initial training. Keep the horse semicollected. Don't let him get heavy on the forehand or strung out behind during the workout. Once the horse is steadily jog trotting, going deep into corners, and bending slightly to the inside of the circle (never use a leading rein to drag the horse around a circle), proceed to brief periods at the road gait; though not speedy, this is faster than the jog trot and retains the same balance. When the horse can perform a road gait without losing form in the corners of an arena, it is time to start training for speed. In the beginning, speed is asked as the horse leaves a corner and starts down a straightaway. Each day ask him to go further into the corner at speed. If he appears unsteady, back off. Don't dwell on speed. The easiest way to ruin a roadster is to push for speed before the horse has attained the muscling, stamina, and balance necessary to retain form. Remember to support and balance the road horse, especially when entering corners, at speed. Once the horse understands and can handle speed, you can change the emphasis. Spend most training sessions between shows working at the jog and road gait.

If possible, prepare the young roadster for his first class by working him in the company of other horses who are performing at speed. Invite a few friends to watch the training session, and simulate the sounds of the show ring with whoops, cheers, and whistles. The atmosphere of the show ring can enhance the attitude and action of the road horse so long as he understands that the sights, sounds, and noise are harmless.

Specific information regarding class specifications for breed-ring show horses (with the exception of the Quarter Horse) can be obtained from the American Horse Shows Association. The American Quarter Horse Association will supply information pertinent to exhibitors of that breed. Other registries will provide the judging standards for their breeds. Information about roadsters can be obtained from the American Road Horse and Pony Association, which promotes this type of horse. (For addresses, see Appendix.)

7

ANTIQUE CARRIAGE COMPETITION

Singles, pairs, tandems, and teams of horses put to vehicles—remarkably like the carriages, coaches, and carts that crowded the streets at the turn of the century—are coming together to fill antique carriage classes at public fairs and private shows. Carefully restored or reproduced wooden-wheeled vehicles, drawn by classic matched horses and driven by a diverse group of enthusiasts, are appearing in number to compete in a division that

Ill. 7-1. A tandem of Friesian horses owned by Frank Leyendekker. The driver is Clay Mair, the groom, Jake Ward.

was once the realm of a small group of nostalgia buffs and carriage collectors. The new group of exhibitors represents a cross section of the equestrian community. Their reasons for entering the once rigidly traditional field are varied. Some competitors find the classes to be an ideal showcase for their horse or breed of horse. Others have discovered in driving an alternative yet fulfilling equestrian pursuit and want to test their skill in public. Still others are enamored of the equipment and want to display a personal restoration project. Whatever the reason, the influx of competitors has made carriage competition a meeting ground for otherwise widely separate interests.

The American Driving Society (the governing body for driving competition in the U.S.), in conjunction with the American Horse Shows Association, has recognized the need for class variety. It has responded with an innovative and appealing roster of classes and promises to broaden interest still more. The original pleasure-driving class (with decided emphasis on turnout), which was the foundation of antique carriage competition for many years, has been relegated to the past. Three categories have taken its place. All are intended to encourage continued interest in restoration and research while inspiring exhibitors to new levels of driving sophistication. The first category, comprised of turnout classes, is primarily for carriage enthusiasts. The lion's share, 70 percent of the 100 point spread—evaluates the impression of the turnout. The remaining 30 points are divided between the horse's performance and the driver's ability.

The second category—working classes—emphasizes the performance of the horse, and awards 70 percent to his performance, the remaining 30 percent of consideration divided between turnout and driver ability.

A third category, reinsmanship, dwells 70 percent of a possible 100 points on driver skill, with turnout and performance of horse contributing 30 percent to overall evaluation.

Each class may be open, or limited to lady, gentleman, junior, or amateur drivers. They can also be separated according to hitch; singles, tandems, and four-in-hands usually compete against their own kind. Most antique carriage divisions also offer obstacle classes to test the dexterity of the horse and driver skill. Large driving shows may include a marathon drive judged on turnout, performance of horse, and competence of the driver. These classes, with their wide range of horse/driver/vehicle combinations, reflect the burgeoning interest in this field of activity.

The Antique Carriage Horse

The antique carriage horse can be any type or breed of horse, but ideally he is a composite of skills. In some ways he is the brilliant and animated breed-ring horse; in others, he is like that steady performer, the combined-driving horse. Good, sound, working conformation and a charismatic attitude are assets. Morgans, Hackney Horses, and Friesians are examples of breeds

Ill. 7-2. A pair of Morgan horses owned by Nemours Morgan Farm and driven by Leslie Kozsely. (Photographer/Budd, Courtesy Martha du Pont)

commonly chosen for antique carriage classes. Their substantial physiques and high, round action add an air of suitability, sparkle, and zest to the turn-out; but many other breeds and crossbreds are equally suitable for certain types of vehicles and classes, despite their less than classic driving conformation. Also, action is not essential. A balanced way of moving that allows true collection and extension is most important. An antique carriage horse should add something, never detract, from the effect of the turnout. For instance, a gooch wagon (a type of phaeton designed specifically for Hackney Horses) is ideally suited for a pair of Hackneys; it would overwhelm a small Arabian, who would be better used to add refinement and beauty to a village cart.

The antique carriage horse is a show horse and should be prepared for appearances in the arena with the same exacting year-round care recommended for breed-ring horses (see chapter 6). Impeccable outward appearance of horses testifies to the owner's dedication and knowledge. Judges and fellow competitors are well aware of the time and energy needed to bring a horse to top condition.

Shoeing for antique carriage horses is not strictly regulated. As a rule, unshod horses are out of place in today's show ring, but, conversely, the use of any obvious gait-altering devices may raise an objection from the judge.

Braiding

Throughout history it has been the custom of horsemen to braid the manes of driving horses. A braided mane highlights the long, elevated, well-shaped neck prized by coachmen. On the other hand, the tails of carriage horses are never braided. This is appropriate only for draft or commercial animals.

Braiding is a tradition, not a rule. The decision whether or not to braid is left up to the individual exhibitor, although it is complicated by the fact that some breed registries require their representatives to be shown with a full mane and tail (Arabians and Morgans, for example). In some instances, a long, full mane that lies neat and flat is more attractive or more correct (for example, with a rustic vehicle). But, like the rider of an unbraided hunter, the driver on many occasions is flying in the face of tradition if he doesn't braid. More and more exhibitors are showing their horses braided, as antique carriage horses rather than as breed representatives.

To prepare a mane for braiding, it must be trimmed or pulled to an average length of 4 inches. The hair is divided into half-inch sections and each section is braided individually. Yarn, string, or ribbon is braided into each plait. Most often the material is the same color as the hair. Or it may be a color that highlights the pin-striping or lining of the vehicle or some other part of the color scheme. It must be subtle, however; it is not intended to add zip or color to the turnout, as is the case with a Saddlebred fine-harness horse. Plan fifteen to twenty braids and cut a 20-inch length of yarn, string, or ribbon for each braid. Clip a narrow bridle path and remove most of the forelock, leaving just enough hair for a single braid. Begin braiding at the top of the neck, behind the bridle path. Fold the length of material in half. Lay the fold against the underside of the hair at the base of the braid. Make a neat, tight plait, including the yarn or string in the braid. Knot the excess material around the end of the braid to hold it together. Proceed down the neck, making small uniform braids. To finish the job, the end of each braid can be drawn through its base and the whole wrapped with the extra yarn or string to hold it in place. Excess ends of material are clipped off. It is not necessary to draw the plaits through their base if they are short. Each may be folded to the underside and tied tightly against the base of the braid. The forelock is braided, folded, and tied in place. Braids should be removed as soon as possible after each day's classes to avoid kinks that will make braiding the following day a chore. Braids seldom stay neat and attractive if they remain overnight.

Equipment

Breast- or neck-collar harness of black or russet color with fittings to match those on the vehicle is correct for antique carriage classes. This type of harness features a broader, more substantial cut of leather than breed-ring show harness or racing harness because the vehicles are heavier. The leather is often lined or doubled and decorated with some patent leather (more if the vehicle is fancy) and decorative stitching. A heavy farm harness is out of place. Harness can also be made ornamental with crests or monograms made of brass or chrome (metal should match vehicle furnishings). These should be very small and inconspicuous to avoid giving the harness a commercial look. A drop, an oval flap of leather that lies on the forehead or in front of the false martingale and is adorned with a monogram, commonly decorates this style of show harness.

Bearing reins and martingales (not to be confused with false martingales) are permitted by the rules, but many judges' opinions indicate displeasure with artificial aids and this is discouraging exhibitors from using such equipment. A sidecheck is considered most acceptable if a bearing rein is necessary. Snaffle bits (half-cheek, eggbutt, or double ring) and curb bits (liverpools, Buxton, elbow curbs) are acceptable. A snaffle or curb bit is correct with a breast-collar harness, but a snaffle is not considered as correct as a curb with a neck-collar harness. Ornate Buxton bits are correct only with formal vehicles.

Harness should be clean, polished, and carefully fitted and adjusted. It should not be so small that the last holes on straps must be utilized or so large that traces or breeching straps must be wrapped several times around the shafts or tied in knots in order to take up excess length. Specialized multiple hitches require additional or unique harness parts. Suit the harness to the horse, the hitch, and the vehicle.

Neck collars are proper equipment for the heavier vehicles and multiple hitches common to the antique carriage division. The neck collar, unlike the breast collar, must fit each horse exactly. There are many variables that must

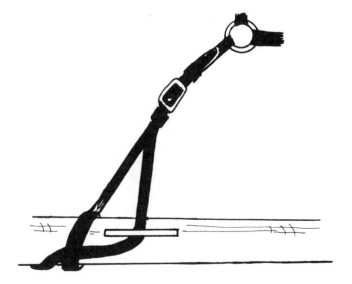

Ill. 7-3.   The breeching strap should not be so long that it has to be wrapped several times around the shaft to take up excess length.

be taken into consideration. The best way to ensure an accurate fit is to try several collars on the horse and to measure the collar that fits. If this can't be done, it is common practice to order the collar using a single measurement. This measurement is an absolutely straight line (don't follow dips and curves) from the base of the windpipe (the dip where the chest ends and the neck begins) to the top of the neck just in front of the withers.

A neck collar should lie flat against the shoulder of the horse and not rock back and forth. It is snug but not tight. A man's finger should fit between the side of the neck and the collar and a man's fist should fit between the windpipe and the base of the collar. The widest part of the collar needs to be at point of shoulder for correct angle of draft. The hames are centered and traces positioned to extend from this point.

One collar will not fit a horse throughout its working life. An aged horse will require a larger collar than a very young horse. An unconditioned horse will need a smaller collar once work has tightened muscles and removed fat. It is important to regularly check the fit of a collar. A poor fit can cause sore muscles and chafe the skin, and it makes work more difficult if the angle of draft is wrong.

Stretch a neck collar against your knee to widen it and turn it upside down before passing it over the head of the horse. Collars are always hung upside down, with the hames removed, to prevent stretching during storage.

Pair Harness

All harness for multiple hitches has two major and several minor differences from single harness. Single horses are hooked between shafts, but horses driven in groups are hitched to either side of a pole or (as is the case with lead horses common to tandems and teams) to arrangements of singletrees (bars) attached to the end of the pole. These arrangements require some variation of harness parts.

The second major difference between singles and groups is the system of coupling reins together. Each lateral group of horses, regardless of total number of horses in the hitch, requires only two reins. The reins coming from the left side of all bits are buckled to the outside left (draught or longer rein of a multiple hitch which travels from the outside of the bit to the driver's hand; the coupling reins are buckled to the draught rein) rein and all right reins are buckled to the outside right (draught) rein.

Basic pair harness for the individual horse is similar to single harness and includes a standard driving bridle, a neck or breast collar and traces, a pad (similar to a driving saddle but equipped with a tug buckle to hold the traces in place), a crupper strap, a crupper, and a breeching or trace holder. A pair consists of two horses hooked on either side of a pole (Ill. 7–3). For a pair, the driver holds two reins in the same manner and uses the same aids as for a single horse. Their traces attach to the splinter bar or to mobile singletrees attached to the bar. The hames of the neck collar, usual on pair harness,

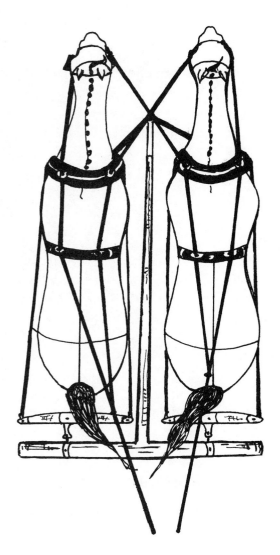

Ill. 7-4. Pair harness.

are held together with a metal kidney link. A ring is put on the lower part of the link. A pole strap or chain is attached to the kidney ring at one end and to a ring on the pole head at its other end. This system, often aided by a breeching or a brake, allows the horses to hold back the vehicle with the pole when going downhill. A false martingale, a strap that attaches between the girth and the base of the collar (buckled around the top half of the kidney link to keep the hames from being pulled off the collar), prevents the collar from riding up when the pole comes forward.

The coupling reins are the shorter of the two pairs of reins. The longer rein is the draught rein. One draught rein is buckled to the outside ring of each horse's bit. A coupling rein is attached to the inside bit ring of each horse. It is threaded through the inside rein terrets on the collar and saddle of the opposite pair horse. The coupling reins are buckled to their respective draught

Ill. 7-5. A tandem of Connemaras driven by Sallie Walrond at the English Connemara Pony Society Show. The vehicle is a skeleton gig. Mrs. Walrond is the author of several books about driving.

reins. The inside rein of the near horse (horse on the left when the driver is seated) buckles to the draught rein of the off horse (horse on the right when the driver is seated). Pressure on this rein applies pressure to the right side of the mouths of both horses. The second coupling rein buckles to the left side of the bit of the off horse and then to the draught rein of the near horse. Pressure on this rein is transmitted to the left side of the mouths of both horses.

Using this basic system, a number of singletrees can be attached to a splinter bar, allowing three, four, even five horses to be hooked abreast and driven with two reins.

Tandem Harness

A tandem, considered by many to be the most difficult hitch to drive, is comprised of one wheel horse (horse closest to the vehicle) and one lead horse (horse in front of the wheeler or at the head of a team). Tandem driving probably originated as a temporary arrangement when extra muscle was needed to pull a heavy load up a steep incline or out of mud. It has evolved to become a respectable test of driver skill since it requires less strength but more delicacy, dexterity, and judgment.

Tandems generally are driven to two-wheeled vehicles and the wheel horse

Ill. 7-6. A tandem tug buckle.

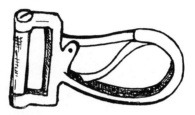

Ill. 7-7. A spring cockeye.

wears traditional single harness—with minor modifications—and is hooked between the shafts in the usual manner. The tug buckles (Ill. 7-6) on the wheeler's saddle have cockeyes (metal loops) extending from their lower sides. These supply a means to hook the lead horse. There are two common methods. In one, the lead horse is equipped with long traces which attach via spring cockeyes (Ill. 7-7) to the cockeye of the tug buckle. In the second method, a tandem bar (a bar resembling a singletree) supported by leather straps which attach to the tug buckles of the wheel horse make long traces unnecessary. The traces of the lead horse are hooked to the tandem bar. The bars of the bit of the wheel horse are joined together to prevent catching on the equipment of the lead horse.

The lead horse may wear a neck- or breast-collar harness which features a simplified saddle. It has no backband or bellyband and no breeching. A strap with a leather loop on each end passes through the crupper strap and hangs over the haunches. The lead traces pass through these loops. The loops (called trace bearers) prevent the lead horse from getting a leg over the trace.

A tandem driver must handle four reins. The leader's reins pass through the usual terrets back to the wheel horse and then are threaded through rosette terrets that project at either side at the point where the browband joins the cheekpieces of the wheeler's bridle. The rein terrets on the wheeler's saddle are called roller terrets (Ill. 7-8); the leader's reins pass through the top half and the wheeler's reins through the bottom half of these terrets.

A random hitch is a variation of tandem driving. Three horses are hitched one in front of the other.

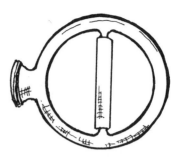

Ill. 7-8.　Tandem roller terret.

Ill. 7-9.　A team. Alan Bristow driving Hungarian Grays at Cricket St. Thomas, England. (Photographer/Ian Brooke/Brooke Photographic)

Team Harness

A team, as defined by British rules, consists of four or more horses and can be called a four-in-hand. (Americans occasionally refer to a pair as a "team".) Two pairs of horses, one in front of the other, make up a four-in-hand. The front pair are the leaders and the pair closest to the vehicle are the wheelers. The off wheeler and leader are on the right and the near wheeler and leader are on the left.

The wheelers of a four-in-hand are hooked on either side of a pole and they wear similar harness with two minor modifications. The bridles of the wheelers feature one rosette terret positioned on the outside juncture of the browband, crownpiece, and cheekpiece of the driving bridle. The pads of the wheelers are equipped with a third or center terret. The draught rein of the off leader is buckled to the near leader's coupling rein and passes through the rosette and center terrets on the off wheeler's harness before arriving at the driver's hand. The draught rein of the near leader is buckled to the off leader's coupling rein and passes through the rosette and center terrets on the near wheeler's harness, then back to the driver.

A metal hook, or "crab," bolts securely to the head of the pole. A main bar, to which are attached two singletrees, or sidebars, is secured to the crab (Ill. 7-10). The traces of the lead horses are hooked to their individual trees, providing a means for them to pull the vehicle. A strap buckles between the end of the hook and the pole, closing the opening, so the main bar can't bounce free. This system, utilizing a crab, main bar, and sidebars, is the basis for a variety of hitches. For example, the five-horse team can feature three leaders and two wheelers; a unicorn has one leader and two wheelers.

Vehicles

Two-wheeled vehicles are the most common and safest for singles and tandems of horses. Four-in-hands and pairs (with the exception of cape carts and curricles) are always put to four-wheeled vehicles. An assortment of vehicles will be on hand for most antique carriage classes, yet despite the appearance of diversity, most vehicles suited to today's competition are of a few basic types. They differ from one another mainly in their ornamentation and superficial body design. With the exception of the lavish, professionally driven coaches that occasionally compete on behalf of affluent stables, the vehicles are usually variations of the following themes: gigs (Ill. 2-8), dog carts (two- or four-wheeled vehicles with louvered compartments under the seat intended for carrying the dogs to the hunt), road or village carts (Ills. 2-9 and 3-13), ralli cars (Ill. 4-2), buggies (Ill. 2-12), surreys (Ill. 5-11), wagons (Ill. 5-10), and phaetons (Ill. 2-13).

All vehicles should be washed, vacuumed, the wood and metal polished, and squeaks and rattles cured (which often entails oiling or replacing washers in the axles), before appearing in the show ring. In fact, the vehicle should be readied with the same care that precedes the presentation section of a combined driving event.

Vehicles are expected to carry "spares kits." Spares are tools used for making emergency repairs. They are mandatory and often useful on marathon drives but only serve to satisfy tradition in the show ring. Vehicles can be equipped with wicker or wooden boxes that are permanently attached or buckled securely in place beneath the seat. These boxes or kits should be neat

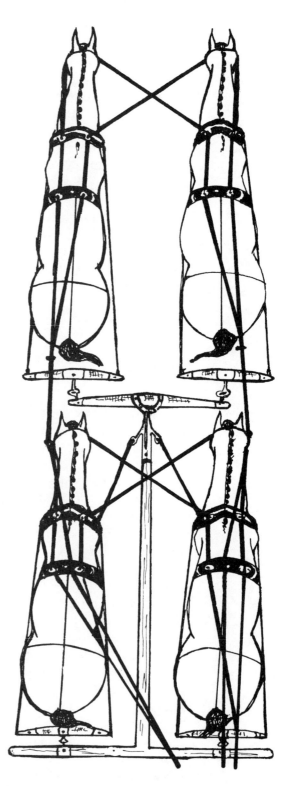

Ill. 7-10.   Team harness.

and large enough to hold the equipment. Each kit must contain a wheel wrench (to fit the axle nuts of the particular vehicle), leather punch, knife, screwdriver, pliers, small hammer, length of rawhide, string or wire, rein splicer or spare rein, trace splicer or spare trace, hame strap if a neck collar is being used; hoof pick; halter, lead, and cooler for each horse.

Old or Used Vehicles

The love of old vehicles is as much a motivating force behind antique carriage competition as is the love of horses and driving. No participant finds it easy to reject an offer or pass up a "good buy" if a remotely serviceable antique vehicle is the object of the bargain. Some parts of vehicles can be easily and inexpensively repaired, but others are hard to come by, and expensive or time-consuming to rebuild. It is a good idea, before becoming involved in a costly, long-term restoration project, to determine the extent of any unsoundness, to weigh projected repair costs against your budget, and to decide the finished value, real or emotional (for example if the vehicle is unusual or perfect for your horse), and then make a decision.

Certain points on the vehicle are crucial and a check of these will give you enough information to make a judgment. The skeleton or frame is the wooden foundation of the vehicle. It should be the first point of consideration. If it is severely damaged, the restoration will be time-consuming if you do it yourself, or costly if you send it to a carriage builder. But the work, whoever does it, is absolutely necessary to serviceability. Broken parts are obvious, but a more subtle adversary is wood rot. Cut or joined edges are particularly vulnerable. Unnaturally soft or spongy wood (it takes the imprint of a fingernail) is rotten and will have to be replaced. Flat, square, or rectangular pieces are not difficult to rebuild, but an ornate or curved support, panel, or dash must be carved or steam-bent. Cracks often are not serious and can be repaired with fiberglass or plastic wood filler.

Metal screws, bolts, and fittings need to be removed and checked for signs of deterioration. All weak or corroded parts will have to be replaced; bent metal that is otherwise sturdy can be straightened.

Wheels are next on the list of points to check. They must be absolutely sound to be safe. Tires, metal rims, and one or two broken spokes can be replaced or repaired without too much trouble. However, cracks, breaks, loose joints, or extensive damage due to wood rot render a wheel unserviceable and beyond repair. Wheels are constructed with special equipment and the special skill of a wheelwright. As demand grows, more and more wheelwrights are appearing to cater to the trade. But their services are expensive.

An axle is another point of stress that is subject to wear. The condition of a common axle can be determined by rolling the vehicle and watching the wheels. If the wheels "run true" (follow a straight line and don't wobble) then the axle is generally in good condition. The axle also can be tested when the

Ill. 7-11. A brougham about to go through an auction.

vehicle is at a standstill by rocking the wheel toward and away from the body of the carriage. There should be a small amount of movement, but excessive play indicates a worn axle spindle that will need to be replaced or reground. Occasionally a loose wheel is the result of a loose hub or worn leather washers. This can be remedied by tightening the hub or replacing the washers. Roller-bearing axles don't wear as quickly as common axles and generally only require replacement of bearings. Bearings are readily obtainable from carriage builders.

Be sure the shafts or pole that are with a vehicle actually fit that vehicle. Obviously, a means to hitch the horse is essential, so if they don't fit (jury-rigging is unsafe) they will have to be replaced. These parts are not difficult to find but their purchase will add to the expense of the project. Cracked poles or shafts can be repaired.

Damaged paint and torn upholstery are superficial problems. Fabric, tools, paints, and varnishes are easy to obtain, and this is one aspect of restoration that doesn't require professional assistance. A layman, utilizing a little patience and foresight, can do the refinishing in a garage or workshop.

Ill. 7-12. The body of a dismantled vehicle awaiting repairs in the workshop of a wheelwright and carriage builder. (Carriage Shop/Have Mule Will Travel)

One more thing to consider before a purchase is the degree of difficulty involved in transporting the vehicle. Light two-wheeled carts can be rolled up a ramp into a pickup truck or towed on a small trailer, but larger, heavier vehicles need a flatbed truck or van to move them from place to place. Some four- and six-horse trailers can be equipped with a transport area for a vehicle behind the stalls, but the size of the vehicle is still limited. Closed transport is always best, and once the vehicle is inside it should be secured in position. Anchor it firmly with ropes or chains and turnbuckles. Wrap and pad any portion of the vehicle that comes in contact with a rope or chain. It is generally considered best to anchor a vehicle by the axles and springs (except fragile C-springs), since ropes rubbing against varnished surfaces may mar the finish. The wheels always should be blocked.

Briefly, a restoration project involves the following steps. Begin with research. Public and private carriage collections as well as libraries are a good source of information. The Carriage Association of America provides an information service to its members on matters of restoration (see Appendix for address). Develop a clear idea of the processes involved and formulate a view of the finished vehicle before proceeding with the actual restoration. An authentic restoration is most painstaking, and every job must bow to subtle dictates of tradition if it is to be successful in the show ring. Such questions as color, style of pin-striping or lining, placement of metal fittings, and inclusion of carriage lamps or crests are determined to some extent by the history of the vehicle.

Every project is different, and steps are skipped or modified to suit the task, but a major restoration follows these steps. First, the vehicle is totally dismantled. Accurate records are kept and each part is labeled with a description of its position in relation to other pieces of the carriage. Samples of the upholstery are saved to aid in matching new fabrics. Then paint and varnish are removed from sections preparatory to replacing or repairing damaged wood and metal parts. Once repairs are finished the vehicle is reassembled. Next, paint and varnish are applied and trim is added. Lastly, the interior is reupholstered and recarpeted. Total restoration can take months, even years, but many carriage enthusiasts consider the results well worth the effort.

The Driver

The clothing of the driver is regulated by rules that govern the antique carriage division. Clothing should be conservative and modern without being faddish. A man should wear a quiet suit, or jacket and trousers, and a hat. Fedoras and derbies are fine hats for rural or sporting vehicles, but more dressy phaetons require a top hat to complete the turnout. Ladies also should adapt their attire to the style of the vehicle and avoid ostentatious adornment. Gloves, an apron or lap robe, a hat, and a whip in hand are required for every driver. Grooms and/or passengers appropriate to the vehicle are allowed to accompany the driver.

Drivers who take part in antique carriage classes drive pairs, tandems, and four-in-hands as well as single horses. Singles and pairs can be driven following the procedures outlined in chapter 4. Tandems and four-in-hands require four reins and some modification of the basic styles of rein handling. It is considered universally correct to hold the four reins "English-style" in one hand (Ill. 7-14). The nearside lead rein goes over the forefinger of the left hand; the offside lead rein passes between the forefinger and the middle finger; the nearside wheel rein is placed beneath and between the same two fingers as the offside lead rein; and the offside wheel rein goes between the middle and third fingers. The thumb doesn't press down on the reins; rather it lies lightly on top. The reins are held firmly in place with closed fingers.

All four reins can be shortened simultaneously, to steady or bring the team to halt, by taking hold of the reins, with the right hand several inches in front of the left hand. The nearside reins are separated by the second finger and the offside reins are grasped by the third and little fingers. The right hand can bring the reins back toward the driver's torso to the degree necessary.

Ill. 7-13. Peter Morin driving a Morgan pair owned by Otterbrook Farm. (Photographer/Bernard Guirey)

To signal a turn, reins can be shortened individually, or by pairs (offside or nearside), using one of three methods. The right hand can grasp a rein or reins a few inches in front of the left hand. The reins are removed from the left hand. The right hand moves behind the left hand and replaces the reins in the left hand. The rein or reins can also be picked up by the right hand behind the left hand and drawn shorter. Or, the reins or rein can be grasped in front and pushed back through the left hand. The reins can be lengthened by reversing any of these procedures.

Some drivers, for example the Hungarians, drive tandems and teams by holding the nearside reins in the left hand and the offside reins in the right hand. The leader's rein is between the index and middle fingers, and the wheeler's rein passes between the third and little fingers. Two-handed driving allows for added sharpness when negotiating sharp or steep turns or changing direction quickly. An obstacle class is an example of a situation where driving with two hands could be an aid. However, most authorities frown on the practice, and some show committees prohibit it in certain classes. Also, it is considered incorrect to use the whip when there are reins in the whip hand.

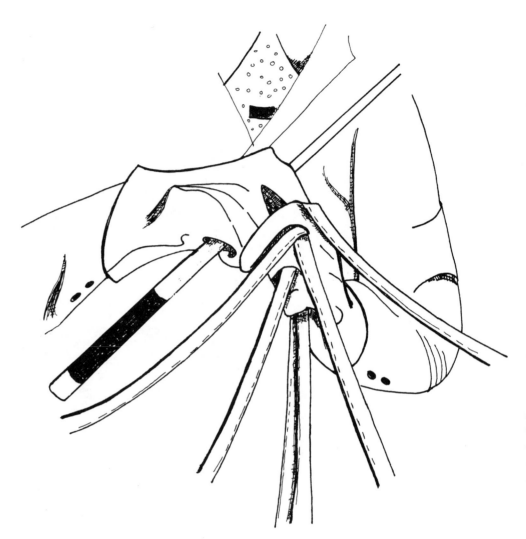

Ill. 7-14. The correct way to hold four reins "English style."

Ringmastership

A good part of showing is the ability to display a horse and vehicle to advantage when the judge is watching. This involves good attitude as well as performance from horse and driver. "Show nerves" are a common syndrome that affects both parties. Preparedness is the best prevention. Don't wait until the last minute. Have everything cleaned and polished well in advance. Hook the horse to the vehicle quietly and calmly. Be sure you allow time for a relaxed warm-up (don't work the horse down—he should be bright) to loosen up muscles. Be in the vicinity of the in-gate prior to the class. A last-minute dash for the gate is disconcerting for all involved. Most judges formulate a lasting opinion as they watch an entry come through the gate and pass along the rail. Don't drift into the ring. The horse should be collected, looking his best, and the driver correctly positioned and self-assured. Stay on the rail when possible. Go deep into the corners. If you must pass, do so in a controlled manner and allow plenty of clearance. Move back on the rail as soon as possible, but never cut close in front of another exhibitor. Follow all official directions for change of gait explicitly, however, don't rush transitions. They are better off belated than imbalanced. Both the horse and the driver should be quiet and attentive in the lineup. Salute the judge after he or she acknowledges your presence. Don't strike up a conversation with your neighbor. Lastly, accept your standings in the ribbons with good grace. It is considered incorrect to approach the judge until after you have finished showing. After your last class it is permissible to seek his opinion, but do so with an open mind.

Special Training

The horses that perform in turnout, working, or reinsmanship classes are expected to perform a walk, collected trot, working trot, extended trot, halt, and rein-back. The horses will perform on the rail in a group or individually off the rail (other exhibitors wait their turn in the lineup). Each of these gaits has been described in chapter 6, on the breed ring, and similar training methods can be used to school an antique carriage horse. However, the carriage horse is not expected to display the height of action, elevation, or flexion common to the breed-ring horse, unless it is a natural result of breeding, conformation, and attitude.

Horses that are shown as pairs, tandems, or teams are judged as a unit. They should be closely matched in size, color, markings, way of moving, and temperament. Minor variations are acceptable. An inch or two of height is not easily discernible if the shorter horse is more upheaded, and it is acceptable to place smaller, flashier, or more active horses in the lead. Each horse should be temperamentally suited to do an equal share of the work; for instance, an eager horse and a sluggard make unhappy teammates. Moreover, each horse should be trained to take any place in the hitch. Horses of a single breed, or close relatives, are easiest to match for multiple hitches.

Horses destined to be members of pairs, tandems, or four-in-hands can be started in harness following the procedure outlined in chapter 3. It is sensible to drive each horse singly until it is at ease with the equipment and relaxed and responsive to the driver. Though no longer a common practice, in the past it was usual for young horses to be hooked for the first time in the company of an older horse. It was thought that a green horse would more easily make the transition into harness if he had the example of a steady horse to guide him. It is a good idea to have one member of a new pair accustomed to being driven in company.

A potential pair should be introduced to one another before they are put to the vehicle. This can be accomplished by ground-driving the animals individually but side by side; they are not attached to each other and a different handler controls each horse. Several sessions may be necessary before the horses work quietly together and are ready to be hooked to the vehicle. The young or green horse should be positioned on the off side, closest to the driver.

The adjustment of the coupling rein is considered one of the most sensitive aspects of a pair or team hitch. The coupling rein has several holes, allowing for a wide range of adjustment, or different adjustments for individual horses. It is important to buckle each rein at a length that keeps that horse straight. If all horses have the same head carriage, then all the reins are buckled in the same hole. But this is seldom the case. All other things being equal, a long-necked horse needs a longer rein than a short-necked horse, and a horse who is overflexing needs a longer rein than one who is pushing his nose out. Also, a horse whose nose is being pulled toward the pole needs a longer rein, and a horse bending his neck to the outside needs a shorter rein. Adjustments of the coupling reins evolve over a period of time as balance improves, equipment becomes familiar, and the horses learn to work together. Ultimately, each horse is set at the length that best suits the individual.

A horse that is accustomed to working as one of a pair or team can develop bad habits which are difficult to correct when he is being driven in a group of horses. He may begin pulling away from the pole, leaning toward a partner, bearing on the bit, or refusing to go up in the collar and do his share of the work. Each horse benefits from weekly sessions in single harness. The specifics of driving—balance, suppleness, and obedience—are easier to teach one-on-one.

Antique carriage classes provide unique, varied, and challenging competition for drivers who are ready to test their skill and an opportunity for those involved with driving sport to come together and exchange ideas. The division also has become a showcase for unique vehicles and fancy hitches, allowing the public a view of advanced driving equipment and techniques.

8

COMBINED DRIVING

Combined driving is the grand prix of harness sport. The three competitions of an event—presentation and dressage, marathon, and obstacle—combine to test every aspect of driving. The cleanliness, general condition, and total impression of driver, vehicle, harness, and horses are scrupulously evaluated during Section I of Competition A: Presentation. The freedom and regularity of paces, harmony, impulsion, suppleness, lightness, ease of movement, and correct position of horses as well as the style, accuracy, and general command of the driver are judged during Section II

Ill. 8-1. HRH the Duke of Edinburgh competing with the Queen's team of Cleveland Bays in the dressage section of an event at Windsor, England. (Court Photographer/Ron Bell, Picture by Press Association)

of Competition A: Dressage. Competition B, the Marathon, tests the fitness and stamina of the horse or horses and the ability of the driver to judge pace and master his animals and equipment. Natural and artificial obstacles can be included in all but the walk section of a marathon. These obstacles provide a uniform test of skill for each competitor. Competition C: Obstacles, determines fitness, obedience, and suppleness of the horses after the relative rigors of the marathon. The foresight and governing ability of the drivers are also measured as they pilot their horses and vehicles through a tricky maze of markers. Viewed as a whole, a combined driving trial is a test of creativity, intellect, and athletic ability—in other words, of driving competence. The sport was not designed as a showcase for bravado, but neither is it a suitable arena for fainthearted drivers or horses.

Combined driving is a young sport. It is still in the process of development, a point underlined by the revision of past rules and the possibility of future changes. The original set of rules was devised as recently as the 1960s when HRH The Duke of Edinburgh was president of the International Equestrian Federation (FEI), the governing body for international jumping, dressage, and three-day event competition. A Polish delegate, Eric Brabec, approached Prince Philip with the suggestion that the FEI develop a set of rules for international driving competition. Prince Philip was skeptical, but feasibility research proved positive. A hearty European driving community was in evidence, although international competition was difficult due to the lack of an unbiased set of rules common to all countries. Sir Michael Ansell was assigned to draw up a set of rules. An outline based on the ridden three-day event was formulated at a conference of European drivers in Berne. The FEI published the first set of combined driving rules in 1969. The original competition, using these rules as a guide, was held in 1970 at Lucerne, Switzerland. In 1971 a first competition took place in England in conjunction with the Windsor Horse Show. The first competition in the United States was held in 1971 and took place in New Jersey. Hungary set the stage for the initial European Driving Championships, which were held in the autumn of 1971. The first World Driving Championships took place in Munster in 1972. World Driving Championships have been held every other year since their inception; the European Championships have been held during the alternate years.

The Combined Driving Horse

The combined driving horse is a paradox. The only restrictions placed on the choice of horses have to do with age and height; horses must be at least four years old and 14.2 (148 centimeters) hands or over (equines under 14.2 hands are classified as ponies). An amazing variety of horses compete at combined driving events. Ex-show horses, Standardbreds who have competed in harness races, and "backyard" pleasure horses find new or additional vocations as combined driving horses. Morgans, Thoroughbreds, Friesians,

Ill. 8-2. Combined Driving Horses. Alwyn Holder driving his team of Welsh Cob geldings through the water hazard at the Cricket St. Thomas Driving Trials in England. (Photographer/Ian Brooke, Brooke Photographic)

and Quarter Horses follow each other, equally capable of success, through the competitions. Any type of horse can be a combined driving horse, but not every horse is a combined driving prospect.

A combined driving horse must be sound in mind and body. A high-strung disposition or excessive docility is as limiting to performance as a straight shoulder or knock knees. The various tests require an attitude that is patient, sensible, willing, yet amply endowed with "heart." The horse should have pleasing conformation and its natural counterpart, good working conformation. He should also have "presence." Presence can be reflected in an ability to perform elegant collected movements and eye-catching extended movements; spectacular high action may improve dressage scores but it will tire the horse during a marathon.

The horse must be physically sound as well; unsoundness is a basis for disqualification. Horses are inspected for soundness on three occasions: before the competitions begin, during the marathon, and before the obstacle test. The horse must be aerobiotically fit and must exhibit strong, toned, well-developed, supple, muscles. In effect, there must be a balance of traits. Too much of a good thing is as detrimental as too little in a multifaceted competition like combined driving.

Equipment

A combined driving harness may be breast or neck collar in black or russet color, equipped with nickle or brass fittings. Above all, it must be in good condition, strong enough to withstand the stress of competition. A fine breed-ring show harness is unsuitable, because it isn't designed with the requisite strength for combined driving. The style, parts, and fittings need to be uniform. The harness should also be correct for the style of vehicle. Bearing reins are acceptable but are seldom used. They are considered an artificial support and should be unnecessary for a finished combined driving horse. Different bits may be used on horses within a pair, tandem, or four-in-hand, but they must be of similar style. The harness can't be altered between presentation and dressage, although a different but safe working harness is acceptable on the marathon.

Vehicles for teams and pairs must have four wheels. A team vehicle, because of its weight (over 600 kg; 270 lbs), must be equipped with a brake. Pair vehicles are allowed a brake or workable system of breeching. Single vehicles may be two- or four-wheeled. No braking system for single vehicles is dictated by the rules, but breeching is recommended. Wood, iron, aluminum,

Ill. 8-3. Combined driving equipment must be strong and is often specially designed for the sport. Louise Serjeant driving a pair of Hackney Ponies to a competition phaeton. (Photographer/Ian Brooke, Brooke Photographic)

and solid rubber tires are acceptable wheel materials; 160 centimeters (63 inches) is the maximum outside width of the wheel track. No part of a marathon vehicle, excepting hubs and splinter bar, can be wider. Wire-wheeled vehicles with pneumatic tires are prohibited unless a special division is offered by the show committee. Antique vehicles are lovely for presentation and dressage, but many are too awkward and fragile for the rough going presented by some marathon courses. Several carriage companies have begun to design competition vehicles that are efficient and painstakingly balanced, with metal wheels simulated to look like wood. (The addresses of some of these companies are given in the Appendix.)

Four-in-hand vehicles must have carriage lamps and rear reflectors on the vehicle during Competition A. This finishing touch, though not required, is recommended for single and pair vehicles that are equipped with brackets. Speedometers and/or odometers are prohibited.

"Spare" equipment is required in every vehicle during all phases of the competition. It includes: (one each) lead trace, wheel trace, lead rein, main bar, lead bar. Pairs, singles, and tandems need: (one each) trace or splice, rein or splice, hame strap if neck collar harness is used, or pole strap for pair harness. Other spares, like a knife, holepunch, and halter, are not required but should be carried on a marathon.

The vehicle should be cleaned and polished before presentation. Leather must be soaped and oiled, and patent leather cleaned with a specially formulated polish. The metal should be cleaned with a metal polish. Seat cushions and carpets must be removed and brushed clean. The interior of the body may be vacuumed. Leather hoods can be cleaned and polished. This is a good time to check spring bolts (oil sparingly with a thin lubricant) and be sure the wheel nuts are tight. Squeaks and rattles can lower the presentation score.

Divisions and Classes

The original combined driving rules were written for teams of four horses, and international competitions still limit entrants to four-in-hands. However, the interests of a broader spectrum of the driving community induced the FEI to enlarge its concepts. The rulebook now states that the same rules can be applied to pairs, tandems, and single horses. These diverse events are popular on national, regional, and local levels. The entrants register in divisions and classes and compete with their peers. The American Driving Society recognizes several levels.

The newest division is "Training Level." It is designed for beginning horses and drivers. The presentation section is waived or judged while the dressage test is performed. A simple training level test is used. Competition B is a marathon without obstacles, and drivers may take a navigator rather than an assigned referee. An abbreviated, simplified obstacle course with increased clearance for all vehicles supplies an introduction to Competition C.

Ill. 8-4. Original combined driving rules were written for teams of four horses, and competitions on international levels are often restricted to teams. Zeuon Szyszkowski driving for Poland at the 1982 World Driving Championships. (Photograph/Courtesy of Driving Digest Magazine)

A second division or level is called Intermediate. This division is limited to entrants who have not won two blue ribbons at a combined driving event above training level. Intermediate horses and drivers must appear for presentation as well as for a dressage test. A marathon consisting of three sections with obstacles is required. Referees are assigned to the vehicles. The clearance allowed between obstacles of Competition C is the wheel track plus 50 cm (approximately 1-1/2-feet).

The highest level is Advanced. A driver must complete three combined driving events, competing at a level above training level, to be eligible for this division. The Advanced level abides by standard FEI rules.

Each division is divided into classes for single horses, single ponies, pairs of horses, pairs of ponies, tandems of horses, tandems of ponies, teams of horses, and teams of ponies. All entrants at training level may compete in one class, but ponies are given slower times on the marathon.

Presentation

Competition A, Section I, is Presentation. It is judged at a halt inside an arena. First impressions suggest it is a beauty contest, though its functions are broader. It judges a driver's ability to turn out his horses and equipment as well as his understanding of driving traditions, but it also ensures that competitors use sturdy equipment and follow effective hooking procedures.

The presentation judge is allotted 50 penalty points for each entrant. These points are subdivided, allowing 10 points for each of five categories: the driver and groom or passengers, the horse or horses, the vehicle, the harness, the overall impression. At the end of the appraisal, points awarded (10—excellent, 9—very good, 8—good, and so on) are added together and deducted from 50, arriving at the remaining number of penalty points. The competitor with the lowest number of penalty points has the highest score.

The driver and the passengers in the vehicle are inspected first. The style of driving is determined by the competitor, but his position should be upright, firm, and assured. The driver must wear a hat, apron or lap robe, and gloves and carry a whip in hand. The clothing should be contemporary, never a costume. The style of vehicle determines the style of dress. Formal dress—that is, a top hat and coat with tails—would look silly on the driver of a road cart. Women's hats should be small, close-fitting, never floppy or adorned with dangling scarfs, veils, or feathers. The gloves are always brown. Shoes should match the color of harness. A whip of correct length and style should be carried in hand. A holly whip with a long thong is correct with neck-collar harness and short thonged whip is suitable with breast-collar harness. The length of stick and thong must be suited to the turnout. The same whip can

Ill. 8-5. Horse, equipment, and driver are judged during presentation. Anita Mellot driving Fancy Lady to a road cart.

be carried in both sections of Competition A, but a different whip is allowed for Competitions B and C. The driver may greet the judge but should not converse except to answer questions.

A four-in-hand vehicle must carry the driver and two grooms during presentation. Pair and tandem vehicles require one groom. A groom is optional for single vehicles. Passengers may be carried during presentation but are not allowed during the dressage test. Grooms should be dressed in stable livery or full livery, depending on the vehicle. A formal turnout requires full livery, that is, tailored jacket with silver or brass buttons (buttons should match the harness furnishings), white breeches, a white stock, black boots with tan tops, and a black top hat. Stable livery can be a conservative dark suit or hunt-seat riding attire. In the first instance, a white shirt, dark tie, and derby are correct. Brown leather gloves are always correct.

The condition, turnout, and cleanliness of the horses also are judged during presentation. The horses should be prepared with the special care outlined for breed-ring show horses. Manes, however, are pulled short and braided. Presentation is the most subjective section of a combined driving competition, and customs vary from place to place. American teams were marked down during the 1982 World Driving Championships because they shaved off the horses' whiskers. This procedure, considered absolutely correct in America, is frowned on in Europe. Hoof care and shoeing also are judged. Generally, hoof paint is less acceptable than a coat of hoof oil, which gives the hoof a healthy shine. Shoeing is not strictly regulated but, in keeping with the spirit of natural methods and clean sport that prevails at an event, gait-altering devices are not acceptable. Horses that are members of pairs, tandems, or teams are inspected for their suitability to one another. They should be so similar in conformation, color, height, and disposition that they appear to be performing as a unit. A variation of a few inches in height can be acceptable if the shorter horse has a higher head carriage. The lead horse of a tandem may be smaller and bolder. Markings may vary slightly.

The vehicle and harness are inspected for structural soundness, cleanliness, and suitability of style. Black harness is considered correct with any vehicle. Brown or russet harness may be used with sporting or natural wood vehicles. The metal furnishings of the vehicle and those of the harness should match. The harness must fit safely; leather straps hooked on the end hole are not considered fully secure. Overly long breeching straps that must be wrapped several times round the shafts are considered incorrect: one circuit of leather round the shaft is ideal. A metal staple must be screwed to the shaft to hold the breeching in position, otherwise it is ineffective because it slides forward. All straps should be threaded through their leather keepers and excess length trimmed by a harnessmaker prior to competition. If a breast-collar harness does not have rein terrets on the hanger strap, it is appropriate to pass the reins under the hanger strap on their way to the terrets on the saddle.

The vehicle is inspected to determine if it is the correct size for the horse or horses and suited to the style of harness. The same vehicle must be used for Competitions A and C, but a different vehicle can be used for the marathon.

Spare equipment is checked during presentation.

The overall impression of the turnout is evaluated before the judge arrives at a score. Scores are posted or announced at the end of the competitions.

Dressage

Dressage is defined as classical training. Its aim is to prepare a horse, by establishing a fundamental education that renders the animal supple, balanced, and obedient for specialized performance. Dressage tests provide a means to evaluate the success of a training schedule. They are written to judge performance at specific levels.

Driving and dressage have always been companionable. European dressage experts have long used the equipment and skills of driving to school horses at all dressage levels. However, there are important differences between ridden and driven dressage. Most obvious, a driving horse does not carry a rider. The forehand of a riderless horse is less encumbered, allowing for lightness and elevation of the forehand, but the loss of the leg and weight aids limits the cues available to the driver. It is generally accepted that the driving horse is less capable of variety of pace and movement than the dressage horse. As some compensation, a driver, unlike a rider, can use his voice to signal the horse during the test.

Ill. 8-6. Combined driving can teach junior drivers judgment and self-discipline. Kendal Williams driving her registered Arabian mare to a road cart.

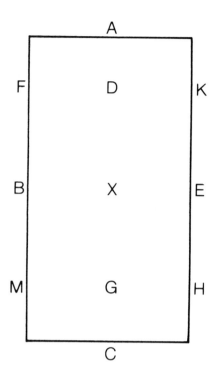

Ill. 8-7. A dressage arena.

The arena for driven dressage is larger than one for its ridden counter-part. An arena for teams must be 100 meters by 40 meters (328 by 130 feet); 60 meters by 40 meters (196 by 130 feet) is considered the minimum dimensions for an arena for singles and pairs. The points around the arena are marked with letters of the alphabet (Ill. 8–7). These letters are used as guides for initiating movements, transitions, and changes of pace called for by a test.

Current driven dressage tests correspond to training and first-level ridden dressage tests, although the inclusion of collected and extended trots and rein-backs gives intermediate and advanced tests some elements of second- and third-level ridden tests. The movements requested can include halt; walk; working, collected, and extended trots; and a rein-back. The halt should be square. During the duration of the halt, the horse or horses must be motionless yet attentive and on the bit. The halt is generally asked for at the beginning and end of the test. The driver is expected to salute the judge during the halt. A man may lift his hat with his right hand (if he is driving with two hands, the right rein must be moved temporarily to the left hand) and briefly and respectfully nod his head before replacing his hat. A female driver does not remove her hat, although she too must nod deferentially. The walk should be brisk, cadenced, and ground-covering. The collected trot is described in detail in chapter 6. However, the emphasis on animation and brilliance allows breed-show horses to wear bearing reins or martingales to support their movements. This type of martingale is considered an auxillary rein and can-

B.H.S. 5 Minute Dressage Test

Time: 5 minutes   Competitor's No. _____

	MOVEMENT	TO BE JUDGED	MARKS 0-10	Remarks
1. A X	Enter at working trot Halt, Salute	Driving in on a straight line Standing on the bit, transition	_____	
2. XCMB	Working trot	Transition, regularity, impulsion	_____	
3. B	Collected trot, circle right 20 metres	Regularity, impulsion, position and accuracy of figure	_____	
4. BFAK	Collected trot	Regularity, impulsion	_____	
5. KXM	Extended trot	Transition, regularity, impulsion	_____	
6. MCHE	Collected trot	Transition, regularity, impulsion	_____	
7. E	Collected trot, circle left 20 metres	Regularity, impulsion, position and accuracy of figure	_____	
8. EKAD	Working trot	Regularity, impulsion	_____	
9. DX	Walk	Transition, regularity, straightness	_____	
10. X	Halt, immobility 10 seconds Rein back 3 metres	Immobility, straightness	_____	
11. XG G	Walk Halt, Salute Leave arena at working trot	Transitions, regularity, straightness, standing on the bit	_____	
12.	Paces	— —		
13.	Impulsion	— —		
14.	Obedience	— —		
15.	Driver	— —		
		TOTAL:		

Ill. 8-8.   The British Horse Society 5-minute Dressage Test written by Sallie Walrond.

not be used for combined driving. A combined driving horse must display natural collection. The appearance and level of collection is dictated by conformation and training. The judge is expected to take these things into consideration. A flashy way of going may never take precedence over obedience. A working trot is faster than a collected trot. The horse is semicollected for this pace, which should appear energetic but not fatiguing. It is a normal trot. For the extended trot, the horse may be semicollected or forward balanced (depending on conformation). The horses are expected to execute long, low, ground-covering strides. A lengthened neck, nose beyond vertical, a long body, and engaged hindquarters provide the physical dynamics for an extended movement. During an extension a horse should not be heavy on the forehand, leave his hocks behind, or lay on the bit. Some information on training for an extended trot is included in the pleasure driving and roadster section of chapter 6. The rein-back is a diagonal, two-beat movement. It must be straight. To achieve straightness, the horse cannot counterflex, brace against the bit with legs spraddled, or move hind legs out of line with the forelegs. (Some information on training a horse to back is included in chapter 5.)

The forward paces (with the exception of the extended trot) are performed as movements. The movements may be a straight line, a circle (20 meters—or 65 feet—is the minimum diameter for a driven circle in current tests), or across the diagonal. Extensions are requested during a change of rein (change of direction) from one corner across the center of the arena to the opposite corner; this allows the longest possible straightaway for building the impulsion necessary to extend. Preparatory to turning the corner, the horses should be driven up and held on their bits on the arena side. After executing the corner, they are allowed to release stored energy into the extension. Transitions should be quick and smooth. Pace and movement must remain constant and consistent until the next transition.

Pairs, tandems, and teams of horses are judged as a unit. The horses are not considered individually.

Horses are not asked to perform lateral movements during driven dressage tests. The position of the driver and the confines of the equipment restrict lateral movement. Of course, a horse can't move a vehicle sideways, but a horse can perform laterally by moving around the vehicle. An example of this type of lateral movement is a "wheel ten," in which the horse transcribes a circle around the vehicle (a two-wheeled vehicle). The horse crosses front and rear legs and performs a sidepass (Ill. 5-9). The vehicle does not move forward or backward, but the horse, pushing against the shafts, causes it to pivot. Teams of draft horses are expected to move laterally. The leaders and wheelers, independent of each other, also are expected to perform lateral movements. Complicated obstacle classes common to draft-horse shows test these skills. Drivers who enjoy cross-country drives are aware of the benefits of lateral movement in harness. This ability can save equipment or prevent an accident. Lateral movement takes place on marathons during negotiation of obstacles. The inclusion of this movement in future dressage tests would give credibility to lateral-schooling theories, spark an exchange of ideas on the subject, and broaden the scope of driven dressage.

The driver is responsible for the accuracy of the movements during the dressage test. It is his or her responsibility to guide the horses through accurate figures, and to do so requires a concept of these figures. A helpful training method requires eight traffic cones and a meter tape. From a particular point, say, point B, measure the perimeter of a 20-meter (65-foot) circle in the dirt of the working arena. Draw an accurate circle, beginning at point B and returning to point B. Set a pair of traffic cones (slightly wider than the track width of the vehicle) spanning the track at B. Set a second pair on the opposite end of a line across the diameter of the circle. Set the other two pairs at opposite ends of a diameter that is at a right angle to the first (Ill. 8-9). Practice negotiating the circle without knocking down the cones. Cones also can be used as guides around corners or to mark the center line.

The paces of a dressage test can be practiced anywhere. A collected trot along a quiet road is one possibility; a brisk extended trot around a track is another. Spend as little time as possible drilling inside an arena. It's boring for the horses. Also, even though a dressage test must be driven from memory, don't attempt to memorize by continually practicing the exact transitions and movements with the horse or horses. They quickly learn to anticipate transitions. And, finally, don't ignore work under saddle. Ridden dressage is excel-

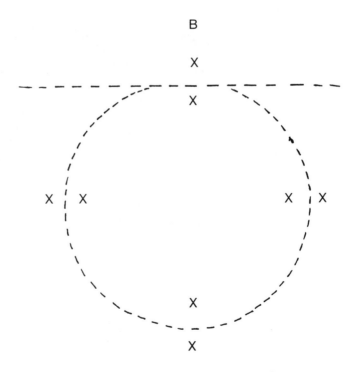

Ill. 8-9. A circle marked with pairs of cones can be used to practice accurate movements.

lent preparation for driven dressage, and a good gallop clears the mind of horse and rider.

In scoring, 150 points are allowed for the dressage test. Each of eleven movements are allotted 10 points, plus 10 points each for the 4 categories under general impression; paces, impulsion, obedience, and the impression presented by the driver. The points awarded are added together and deducted from 150 to give the number of penalty points. The driver with the lowest score of penalty points is the winner. The scores for Section I and Section II are added together to arrive at the score for Competition A.

The Marathon

The marathon, a cross-country drive, is the most important competition of a combined driving event. It is possible to accrue more penalty points during this phase than during the others combined. It is so crucial that tie scores for the entire event are resolved in favor of the competitor with the best score on the marathon.

The marathon is designed to judge the stamina and fitness of the horses and the ability of the driver to judge pace. Maximum average speeds are ascertained for predetermined distances along a course mapped over country

Ill. 8-10. The Marathon. Gyorgy Bardos driving for Hungary at the World Driving Championships in Holland, 1982. Mr. Bardos was twice World Driving Champion. He placed second at Apeldoorn. (Photograph/Courtesy of Driving Digest Magazine)

roads and tracks. Competitors are given penalty points for completing distances faster or slower than the time allowed (though the rules do not prescribe penalties for faster times in the walk sections or section E) as well as for other breaches of rule etiquette.

A standard marathon, following FEI guidelines, consists of five sections called A, B, C, D, and E. The pace, maximum distance, and average speed is published by the FEI and, with some modifications, by the American Driving Society. The pace for each section of every marathon is stipulated as follows: A = trot, B = walk, C = trot, D = walk, E = trot. The course cannot be longer than 27 km (16¾ miles). The course designer, working within the published framework, decides the actual distance and average speed for each section. Abbreviated marathons are designed for the training level and intermediate divisions of a combined driving event.

All sections of a marathon are marked with pairs of red and white flags called gates. These are spaced at regular intervals and each competitor must pass between every pair, in order, with the red flag on the right and the white flag on the left. Passage between gates is recorded on an official scoresheet by the referee, who rides in the vehicle. Gates prevent drivers from taking shortcuts. Once a pair of flags has been negotiated in the right direction it may be reentered from the opposite direction if necessary though there would seldom be a need to backtrack.

Ill. 8-11. A water hazard. Mrs. K. Bassett driving four skewbald geldings to a surrey on the marathon at the Cricket St. Thomas Driving Trials. (Photographer/Ian Brooke, Brooke Photographic)

Ill. 8-12. 1, One way to negotiate a marathon obstacle. Mrs. R. Hancock driving a Welsh cob to a competition vehicle at Bicton Driving Trials, Devon, England. (Photographer/Ian Brooke, Brooke Photographic)

Ill. 8-13. 2,

Ill. 8-14. 3,

Sections A, C, and E can contain hazards—such as rough terrain, water crossings, or grades—that are part of the countryside. More devious tests or "obstacles" are an essential part of Section E. These are constructed and should appear indigenous to the locale. Each obstacle is surrounded by a clear but unobstrusive line. Inside the marked circle is the penalty zone. A vehicle is timed from the moment the nose of the horse (or horses) crosses the line until the last portion of the carriage moves outside. Inside the penalty zone is a series of flagged gates. Each competitor must pass through the gates in correct sequence before leaving the zone. 1 penalty point is scored for each commenced period of 5 seconds, including the first 5 seconds (incidentally, there is a strong feeling this should be changed to 1/2 penalty for each second in the hazard). A maximum of 5 minutes is allowed. Overtime means elimination from Competition B.

The marathon is less formal than the other competitions. A driver may wear comfortable, less traditional, clothing. Aprons, lap robes, and gloves are optional. A whip in hand is required. A driver is penalized for handing the whip to another person, although the groom may hand a spare whip to the driver if the original is lost or broken.

Vehicles for teams must carry at least four people. Pairs, tandems, and singles carry two. These totals include the driver and referee. Grooms are not required to wear livery on the marathon. Vehicles should carry the equipment recommended for cross-country drives (chapter 5) for use in case of breakdown.

The function of the marathon is two-fold: judging the strength and stamina of the horses as well as the ability of their driver to determine pace and distance. Since conditioning of the horses must take place prior to the event, the problem of the moment is the ability of the driver to devise a system to monitor distance and time. Some of this work must be done at home. A driver needs to know the speeds of his horses at their various gaits. Measured distances should be routinely covered and timed at the walk and trot, using the identical equipment that will be used on the marathon. Rough ground, grades, and deep footing should also be evaluated to determine how they affect overall speed.

Only with a working knowledge of the capabilities of the horse (or horses) can a driver devise a scheme for the marathon. He or she should measure the course, pinpointing obvious landmarks, and draw a chart. The chart can be clipped to the dash during the marathon. Variations of the course must be marked on the chart, especially areas where time can be lost or made up. The speed allowed is an average speed. Sometimes the pace will be faster, sometimes slower; the challenge is to arrive within the allotted time. Horses cannot change pace within a section without accruing penalty points, except in rare areas marked "any pace." The approach and route through the gates of each obstacle also must be considered and charted; if any gate is missed, elimination, from Competition B, ensues. It is important to make these calculations beforehand and be able to concentrate on the business of driving during the marathon.

The competitor with the fewest penalty points is the winner of the marathon.

Conditioning for the Marathon

A horse who performs a marathon must be strong, fit, and athletic. It is the moral responsibility of a driver to prepare his horses. Compulsory halts (including veterinary inspection and examination) are mandatory after Sections D and E. Often, despite this precaution and despite the rule that "exhausted horses must be eliminated," horses are entered that do not have the stamina to compete.

Conditioning is a process that prepares the body to use more oxygen and thus fuel the system for increased performance. A physiological result of conditioning is that the blood carries more red cells to the muscles and removes waste more efficiently. The driver can chart and gauge this process by taking the heartrate of the horse. A normal equine heart (at rest) beats between 26 and 40 times per minute. During a workout, the pulse rate of a unfit horse will stay below 120. The heart of a fit horse will beat closer to 150 times per minute. This horse can work steadily for at least two hours, because the heart is efficiently moving blood to and from muscle cells. Recovery time is another guide to fitness. A fit horse, after five or ten minutes of walking, will drop back to a heartrate that is half of the "at work" rate. High pulse rates

Ill. 8-15. Horses must be conditioned for combined driving. Anita Mellot driving Fancy Lady to a road cart.

(over 150) or pulse rates that do not return to normal within a reasonable amount of time indicate too much stress, too soon. Accurate records of heart-rate should be kept throughout a conditioning program. The rate should be taken before a workout (at rest), during the workout, and after the horse has been walked for five or ten minutes following a workout. Pulse rates can be taken efficiently with a stethoscope. Heartbeats are counted for 15 seconds and multiplied by four to arrive at the rate per minute. Pulse can also be taken manually. The mandibular artery runs below the jawbone. Find this artery with a finger (don't use a thumb, since a strong pulse in the thumb interferes with an accurate count of the pulse of the horse). Press the artery against the jawbone. Other arteries can be used to count pulse, but they are more difficult to find and harder to read. One runs along the neck, in front of the withers; others are the digital arteries that pass over the sesamoids on the outside of the foreleg.

Monitor carefully. If the pulse rate goes above 150 or does not drop back to near normal rates within a reasonable time after a workout, something is wrong with the program. Evaluate the schedule while allowing the horse to return to a less strenuous level of training. Two or three days of rest in a paddock or pasture may be necessary to restore a healthy attitude that you may have overlooked in your concentration on physical conditioning. This program can't be rushed. Each horse must be taken at his own speed.

It takes six to nine months, depending on the age, health, and previous exercise schedule of the individual horse, to condition a horse for serious competition. This does not mean you can't show in a training-level division, but suit the demands to the preparedness of the horse. Long, slow, distance training (LSD) is univerally acknowledged to be the intelligent basis for a conditioning program. The horse is gradually, but steadily strengthened and his aerobic capacity enlarged by progressively increasing the strenuousness as well as the length of daily workouts. Where to begin depends on the horse. A youngster out of pasture, an ex-show horse, and a fat aged horse need different schedules. The average horse requires thirty to sixty days to reach the point where strenuous workouts can be incorporated into the program. This horse can begin with thirty-minute workouts (six days of work, one day of rest per week). Plan sessions of walking, with brief intervals of trotting, the first week. The horse can be longed, ground-driven, long-lined, or driven during the workouts. Use pulse and recovery periods as a guide to increase the number and length of the intervals at the trot. Always warm up at the walk, work down at the walk, and provide recovery periods at the walk. Work up to hour-long sessions and incorporate some cantering (on the longe or under-saddle) by the third week. Go slow. The object of LSD is to improve the elasticity of connective tissue, to build muscle, and to increase stamina by strengthening the cardiovascular system. It takes time.

At the end of six or eight weeks, strenuous workouts can be substituted for LSD two or three times a week. This type of conditioning requires short periods of stressful work. It develops strength and stamina. This method is commonly used to condition race horses and is called "overdistance" training. Strenuous workouts should be demanding but short, while alternate workouts are long and slow. Gradually increase demands on the horse. Short gallops under saddle can be a beginning. Practice extended trots cross-country, trotting up and down grades, or brisk trotting patterns that incorporate numerous changes of direction (figure eights, serpentines, circles), inside an arena. Twice a week, aim for a pulse rate near 150 and maintain it for thirty minutes. Continue to religiously record pulse rates before, during (at regular intervals), and after training sessions. Be prepared to drop back to an easier schedule if the horse shows signs of being overly stressed.

Two signs, other than heartrate, can be used to judge the success of a conditioning program. The normal respiration of a conditioned horse is eight to twenty breaths per minute. A blowing horse can breathe as fast as ninety breaths per minute. The conditioned horse will return quickly to a normal respiration rate after strenuous work. The quality of sweat provides another cue. The sweat of an unconditioned horse is thick, gummy, and odorous. The sweat of a conditioned horse is thin and watery.

A third level of conditioning, called "interval training," is important for horses that must work at speed, horses that race in harness, for example. Interval training adds speed workouts to the program. The bursts of speed (always preceded by a warm-up and followed by a recovery period) shock the system into working at optimum efficiency and help develop strength to do so on a regular basis. Speed is not essential to the combined driving horse. "Long, slow, and distance" training is sufficient for their needs. (Interval training will be discussed in chapter 9, "Harness Racing.")

Obstacles

The last, but nonetheless exciting, competition of a combined driving event is an obstacle test. Drivers pilot their turnouts between pairs of markers set barely wider than the wheel track of their vehicles. Easily dislodged balls are perched on top of the markers. Penalty points are accumulated by knocking or dislodging markers or by moving slower than a predetermined time that is based on the distance to be covered and the number of horses in the turnout.

The competition is designed to test horses' performance after stress (the marathon) and to measure driver ability to judge distance and maneuver his horses and equipment. Obstacles are arranged in a specific pattern and must be entered in a posted order. Each set of markers is arranged to be a uniform

Ill. 8-16. Driving the obstacle test. Dr. Peter Anderson driving Welsh Ponies in tandem at Bicton. (Photographer/Ian Brooke, Brooke Photographic)

Ill. 8-17. Driving obstacles at the World Driving Championships, 1982. Ysbiand Chard driving a Dutch warmblood team for Holland. (Photograph/Courtesy of Driving Digest Magazine.)

Ill. 8-18. Combined driving offers new horizons for horses and drivers. Gayle Warren driving Arabian, Mon-Bo, to a road cart.

distance wider than each individual competitor's wheel track. The obstacles are measured and readjusted between tests to assure fairness and accuracy. Competitors may walk the course before competition. This provides an opportunity to devise a plan of approach and to support memory with actual experience.

Practice at home is the best training. Traffic cones topped with tennis balls make good markers. These can be placed in arrangements that incorporate single or multiple (serpentine) pairs of markers per obstacle. Ground poles can be used to construct more difficult (U- and L-shaped) obstacles as dexterity increases. Course designers are ingenious, so be experimental. It is generally agreed the best approach to a pair of markers requires the horse and vehicle to be straight. Much planning and foresight are required for a tight course to avoid being penalized for circling before an obstacle, stopping, backing, or crossing one's own track. Hone your judgment before working for speed. If the approach is correct, speed is an easy addition, but correcting a misjudgment at speed is another matter.

The young sport of combined driving is opening new horizons for drivers and horses. No longer must the show horse end a career at eight or ten years of age because youthful good looks are fading; nor must the Standardbred who lacks speed be retrained as a riding horse because he has no future in harness. If drivers are bored with the railwork common to the breed ring, combined driving gives them a place to go, beyond local tracks and fields. Combined driving promises to take harness sport to new levels of sophistication.

Specific rules for combined driving can be obtained from the Fédération Equestre Internationale, the American Driving Society, and the American Horse Shows Association. The American Driving Society also offers a combined driving organizer's kit.

9

HARNESS RACING

Although the sport of racing in harness is as old as man's association with the horse, until recent times activity was limited by awkward equipment and a lack of suitable racing surfaces. Earliest heats were probably informal. Many were brief sprints between neighbors vying for the right-of-way on a local path or road. Speed of horse and driver skill determined the winner then, as it does now.

Today, harness racing is a modern industry that has great appeal for spectators as well as for participants. Light, safe, fiberglass sulkies, nylon harness, plastic hobbles, all-weather tracks, effective night-lights, and efficient computerized communications have revolutionized the sport, increasing popularity and involvement on all levels. No longer is the harness race a sporting exchange between two New England farmers to provide an afternoon's entertainment for their friends. It is a year-round national pastime, attracting more viewers than any other driving activity. And its popularity is not limited to the United States. Harness racing has an enthusiastic following in such countries as Russia, Hungary, Italy, France, Australia, New Zealand, and Canada.

The Race Horse

Harness racing is so specialized that only one breed of horse, the Standardbred, possesses the speed to compete. The Standardbred averages between 14.2 and 15.3 hands, is generally bay or brown, and weighs between 900 and 1,150 pounds. The breed is not noted for an esthetically pleasing conformation, but more than a hundred years of selective breeding have produced a functional and powerful body, and when performing, "flying" at a trot or pace, the Standardbred is beautiful to see.

All Standardbreds share a common ancestor, a Thoroughbred named Messenger whose ancestry shows a heavy infusion of Arabian blood. He was never raced at a trot and seems an unlikely foundation sire for a trotting breed, but one of his sons sired Hambletonian. This horse, number 10 in the register of the breed, was out of a trotting-bred mare. Hambletonian sired over a thousand offspring, and all male Standardbred lines trace back to him. He is considered the source of the breed's speed and success. Other breeds of horses, notably the Morgan and the Canadian Crossbred, were crossed with horses

168

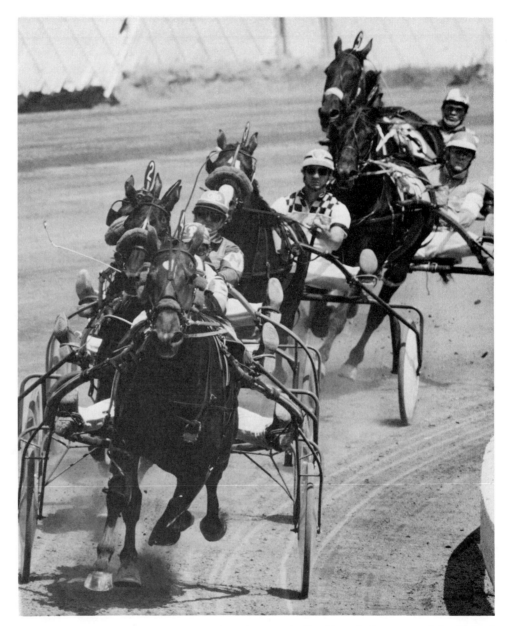

Ill. 9-1. Harness racing. (Photographer/George A. Smallsreed, Courtesy of the United States Trotting Assn.)

of Hambletonian descent, improving the breed decade by decade thoughout the 1800s until the books were closed.

Originally, a horse could not be registered as Standardbred unless it could trot a mile in 2:30. This qualifying time was called the "standard," and this term eventually was adopted as the breed's name. Today Standardbreds routinely trot or pace the mile in 1:55. Outstanding individuals cover the distance in less time. Examples are Lindy's Crown, who trotted the mile in 1:54.4, and Niatross, who paced the mile in 1:49.1. These speedy horses are moneywinners too. The trotter Savoir earned $1,365,145 and Niatross earned $2,019,213. Standardbreds also are enduring. Rambling Willie, winner of over a million dollars, was still winning at the pace at age twelve.

Standardbreds often are purchased as yearlings, started in harness at the end of their yearling year, and raced as two-year-olds. Assessing the potential of so young a horse is always a risk, but it can be an educated guess. Most respected trainers agree that a knowledge of pedigree is essential. The offspring of horses who were successful on the track, or the progeny of horses who have been known to produce winners, are better bets than unknowns. Still, a pedigree is just a piece of paper; the horse must also have good working conformation.

As a rule of thumb (though there are exceptions to every rule), the ideal Standardbred race horse averages around 15.1 hands. His head has a straight nose and good width between the eyes, because "brain space" translates into intelligence, good sense, and manners. A flat nose and clear, round eyes are an indication of the good frontal vision necessary for maneuvering on a crowded track. An aerobic system of great capacity is needed for speed, that is to say, a large heart and lungs and open air passages to get the air to the organs. Horsemen, therefore, look for a broad chest, wide heart girth, long neck, and good width (four fingers of a man's hand should fit side by side between the jawbones) between the jawbones and large nostrils. Straight legs are a must. The speed at which the legs of a race horse move multiplies the liability of any deviation from the norm. Legs that are not straight can interfere or overreach and place undue stress on ligaments, tendons, muscle, and bone. A deep (at an angle to the body), sloping symmetrical shoulder, sloping pasterns, and well-shaped hooves are essential to give spring and power to movement and also to act as shock absorbers. The angle of all three should be similar and never straight. A straight shoulder, straight pasterns, and a steeply angled hoof indicate that the horse pounds rather than springs against the ground. Lastly, the hindquarters should be muscular and the hips level. The hindquarters may be higher than the withers (Hambletonian's haunches were 2-inches higher). Oldtimers consider this trait to be a portent of speed.

Special Care

Standardbreds are raced routinely as two-year-olds and are expected to handle a rigorous full schedule as three-year-olds. Thus, they must be exposed to the maximum stress of training while they are still in an early stage of growth and development. The feeding program of race horses must supply nutrients that quickly convert into energy to meet strenuous daily demands. Each horse is an individual and feed must be adjusted to satisfy special needs. But the average Standardbred—like the breed-ring horse or the combined driving horse—must have grain in addition to hay to meet energy demands. Starch, present in grain, is converted to energy more quickly and more efficiently than cellulose, which is the primary unit of hay. An average race horse receives 15 to 20 pounds of hay and 9 to 12 pounds of grain per day. Water, free-choice salt, and a vitamin-mineral supplement are also necessary. These horses are fed three times a day. The largest portion is usually given in the evening, though it is generally no more than 25 percent larger than the morning or midday ration. The horses receive half of their normal amount of feed on days when they do not work. It is also considered important to feed a horse at the same time each day. A valuable trotter fretting in his stall because his dinner is late can injure himself. It is never worth the risk.

Race horses are athletes. They are expected to perform at peak routinely during training sessions and races. As much special care must be given to "bringing them down" after a race as was given to preparing them for it. The horse is unhooked and led to a place sheltered from wind and drafts where he is sponged with cool water and allowed to swallow a few mouthfuls of water. Then he is bathed with warm water. Some grooms hose off their horses, others prefer to sponge them down from a bucket to which has been added a tablespoon of liniment—or liniment and vinegar—or salt. Liniment, a brace, is refreshing. It opens the pores, tightens the skin, and is supposed to temporarily relieve muscle stiffness or soreness. Salt is an antiseptic. A sweat scraper is used to remove some excess water from the coat, followed by a squeezed-out sponge to take up some more. The horse is then rubbed with rags or towels to remove the remaining moisture. The animal is covered with a skim sheet (warm weather) or a cooler (brisk weather), which is secured across the chest with a blanket pin or cooler clip to keep it from gapping open. The horse is walked until cool and dry if weather permits. If it is too cold, the horse is rubbed in the stall until he is cool and dry. The groom works on one part of the body at a time, folding the cooler back as he proceeds. The horse is allowed to sip water every ten or fifteen minutes throughout this process. A horse is cool when his respiration has returned to a normal sixteen to twenty breaths per minute, his hair is dry, his body is cool, and he refuses water. Depending on the temperature and humidity of the day, as well as on the strenuousness of the horse's exercise, cooling out takes one and a half to two hours. The horse is then returned to his stall.

Race horses often are trained or raced in heats, with generally less than an hour between heats. The horse is not cooled down during this time, but he is allowed to recover. He is unharnessed and lightly sponged with cool (never warm) water. The cool water refreshes but does not relax the horse. Every ten or fifteen minutes he is allowed to drink. The horse is covered with a cooler to keep his body warm and moist. He stands in his stall, with limited access to water, and wearing the cooler, until it is time for the next heat.

Shoeing is of special consequence to race horses. They must travel straight and true to perform at optimum speeds. Length of toe, angle of shoe, and shoe weight are carefully gauged and adjusted throughout an animal's career.

Ill. 9-2.   Race horses are athletes who are expected to perform at peak on demand. (Photographer/George A. Smallsreed, Courtesy of the United States Trotting Assn.)

John F. Simpson, Sr., in *Care and Training of the Trotter and Pacer*, describes the process as a "delicate science of inches and ounces." To complicate matters further, the different gaits of the trotter and pacer (the trotter moves diagonally and the pacer moves laterally) require different shoeing emphasis for balance. The trotter is expected to move in front with a round, bold stroke and folded knee, bringing the hoof 2 or 3 inches below the elbow at the top of the movement and flinging it out with great extension at the bottom of the movement. The hind legs of the trotter display less height of action but more driving extension. A pacer moves lower to the ground in front and wider behind. The ideal trotter wears a 3-1/2-inch toe and a 48-degree angle in front; toe length behind is 3-1/4-inch and the angle 54 degrees. The ideal pacer has a 3-1/4-inch toe and 50-degree angle in front, with a toe length of 3-1/8-inches and an angle of 54 degrees behind. These are averages and much variation of these measurements occurs.

Most horsemen aim for the shortest toe possible to balance the horse. It takes less leverage to pick a hoof of small diameter off the ground than one of large diameter, and thus there is less stress on the ligaments and tendons of the leg. Despite this fact, a long toe is often necessary; it acts as a

Ill. 9-3. Trotters move diagonally and require different shoeing emphasis than pacers. (Artwork/Courtesy of the United States Trotting Assn.)

stabilizer to the hoof in flight and can straighten crooked movement.

The angle of the hoof determines the way it will hit the ground. A steeply angled hoof jars or pounds, while an excessive slope brings the horse down on his heels, stretching the connective ligaments of the leg. The correct angle permits the horse to contact the ground with his weight well distributed across the structure of the hoof, allowing the sole, hoof wall, and heels to expand and contract as nature intended, absorbing the concussion of the stride.

The main function of the shoe is to protect the hoof, but it can also be an aid to balance, affecting the speed, fold, and extension of the leg. These things are accomplished by varying shoe weight, shape, and surface. Shoes for race horses are generally steel or aluminum and weigh between 5 and 12 ounces; variation is possible in the shape of their parts (oval, round, curved, or square). They may have projections (chocks) or grooves on the outside. Shoe weight, like toe length, can be used to modify the position and speed of the hoof in action. Shoe shape aids the hoof in flight by redistributing weight. Besides chocks and grooves, there are trailers, bars, and other variations that can be used to slow down or speed up the hoof as it leaves the ground. Since pacers have shorter and smaller hooves than trotters, their shoes are smaller and thus lighter than those worn by trotters. The race horse must be reshod every three or four weeks to keep him perfectly balanced at all times. A misstep can cause a serious injury when a horse is moving very fast.

Grooms, Trainers, and Drivers

Three people are essential to the upkeep, training, and racing of the Standardbred: the groom, the trainer, and the driver. The groom is the only unlicensed member of the group, but he is with the horse more and is probably the most important of all to the welfare of the animal. The groom has charge of daily care. He does the feeding, cleans the stall, grooms, harnesses, assists in hooking and unhooking, cools the horse down after workouts, cleans the tack, and maintains a vigil in the event of injury or illness. It is often a twenty-four-hour-a-day job and excellent training for anyone who wants to be a professional horse trainer or driver.

The trainer is responsible for overseeing the racing stable. He is in charge of starting young horses in harness as well as training, conditioning, shoeing, and mandating daily care for all horses at his stable. He also plans race schedules and manages the grooms. A trainer must be licensed by the United States Trotting Association (USTA) if he or she expects to work at tracks within their jurisdiction. To obtain a license, an applicant must prove good moral character, be eighteen years of age or older, furnish a completed application form with photographs, submit evidence of an ability to train horses and manage a racing stable (this evidence must include at least three years working as a groom or second trainer), pass a written and physical examination, submit fingerprints, and pay a small fee. These requirements are designed to safeguard the integrity of the harness racing industry.

The person who drives the race is the driver. Unless he is also the trainer,

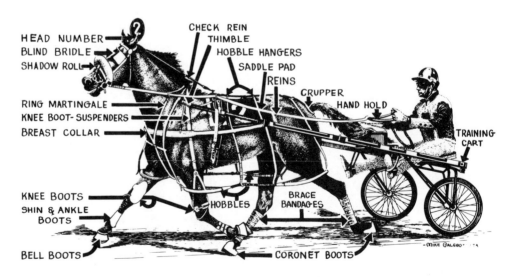

Ill. 9-4. Equipment commonly worn by the pacer. (Artwork/Courtesy of the United States Trotting Assn.)

he spends little time with individual horses (a driver can be a trainer, but he must have a license for each activity). A topnotch driver may participate in races at different tracks on the same day. His job is to elicit top speed from a trained horse and to drive a safe and strategically sound race. For each race the driver wears the colors of the stable to which the horse belongs. These are specific combinations of colors, registered with the USTA, that enable track officials and spectators to tell the horses apart. The driver's safety helmet and jacket as well as the saddle pad and number card of the horse exhibit the stable colors. The qualifications for a driver's license are less stringent than those for a trainer's license, but there is one important difference. A driver must prove he has at least 20/40 vision (it may be corrected) in both eyes, or if he is blind in one eye, 20/30 vision in the remaining eye.

Some licenses allow drivers and trainers to participate only in certain activities, such as in matinee (afternoon) races, amateur races, fairs, or qualifying races. A provisional license is granted for an interim period prior to receipt of the all-encompassing "A" license.

Equipment

Most horsemen agree that a naturally straight, balanced, and gaited horse is esthetically pleasing and a superior prospect as a race horse. It may seem strange, then, that standard harness-racing equipment appears so complicated and inhibiting. Boot, poles, and hobbles, plus a harness and sulky are routine accouterments for trotters and pacers, yet these horses continue to move down the track at ever increasing speeds. The reason for all the equipment is two-fold. First, the "natural" horse is rare; and second, the common practice of racing gangling, growing youngsters necessitates a system of aids. Each piece of equipment has its function: to improve balance, to keep the horse straight and true to gait, or to protect the horse by preventing injury to himself or others in the race. The equipment is not regulated; it is adapted by the trainer to suit each horse. And it is reasonable to assume that knowledgeable trainers, whose livelihoods depend on top performance from carefully nurtured horses, are not going to indulge in counterproductive practices.

The racing harness includes most of the basic harness parts. The bridle may be open or closed and is worn with a noseband. Pacers commonly wear closed bridles, and trotters open bridles, but there are many exceptions to the rule. The bit may be any of a wide variety of half-cheek driving snaffles (Ill. 2–4) or ring snaffles used in conjunction with a check bit. An overcheck bearing rein is used. The breast collar is usually equipped with short traces that buckle to trace hooks on the outside of the sulky shafts. A lightweight saddle equipped with wrap straps, a crupper strap, and sewn crupper (a buckled crupper can snag a rein), plus reins with hand holds, complete the harness. The race harness is strong but light, and generally black with nickle or stainless steel hardware.

Ill. 9-5. Overcheck bits are usually straight bar or jointed bradoons.

The shadow roll is a tube of sheepskin—though it can be a brush—that many horses wear in addition to the bridle. It is positioned between the eyes and the lips (must never interfere with the bit) and buckles under the chin. The shadow roll prevents the horse from seeing the track directly in front of him but does not interfere with his line of vision straight ahead. Its function is to stop horses from shying at shadows or dark spots on the ground or at papers blowing across their path. A horse who jumps sideways during a race can cause an accident.

A head pole is another common piece of equipment. This is a telescopic rod that buckles to the saddle, extends along the horse's neck, and attaches to a head halter. It can be used on the right or left side. The function of the head pole is to keep the head straight, since a horse who carries his head or haunches to one side is difficult to steer and often breaks gait. A gaiting strap, a piece of leather stretched taut between a shaft and the crosspiece of the cart, is used to keep the haunches straight.

Boots for trotters and pacers occur in amazing variety. Whatever part of the front and hind leg needs protection, there is a boot that does the job. Boots commonly are used in unison with one another. It is the straps or suspenders needed to hold them in place that give race horses the appearance of being overdressed. Though generally used for protection, some boots worn by trotters on their front legs are used to improve balance and gait.

Hobbles are an aid worn by pacers. Usually they are constructed of plastic or nylon and encircle the legs on each side above the knees and hocks. Straps connect the loops on each side to one another and additional straps buckle around the neck and over the back to hold the hobbles in place. The pace is an "acquired gait," and hobbles are necessary to keep the horse from "mixing gaits," that is, from breaking into a more normal trot. Hobbles also balance or steady the horse by giving him some support when he is moving very fast.

Martingales are straps that fasten around the girth and extend between the front legs. A standing martingale is a single strap which attaches to a ring on the head stall. A running martingale separates into a fork of leather with a ring on each end. The driving reins are threaded through the rings between the ring terrets on the saddle and the bit. A standing martingale keeps the horse from moving his head above a certain point. A running martingale provides the driver with additional control by allowing more leverage on the bit, although it should be adjusted so that there is little downward pull on the lines. It also holds the bit in place.

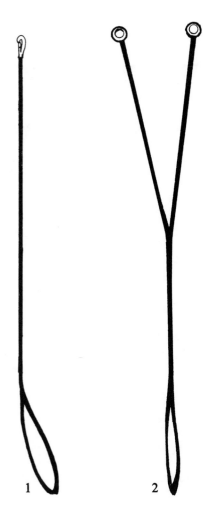

Ill. 9-6. Martingales:
  1. Standing martingale
  2. Ring or running martingale

A horse who gets his tongue over the bit during a race can lose speed; even worse, the pain may cause him to veer to one side. For this reason, tongue ties or tongue controllers are commonly used on race horses. This device may be a simple piece of fabric that passes over the tongue and ties under the jaw, a rubber or leather strap that buckles under the chin, or a metal double-U with a special leather carrier. The tongue must by lying flat in the mouth when the controller is put in place; the device should never be tight enough to cut off circulation.

A kicking strap is used if the horse has a tendency to kick (Ill. 3-15). This piece of equipment is described in chapter 3.

Trainers and drivers use two types of vehicles—training carts and racing sulkies. A training cart has wooden shafts, a metal undercarriage, and

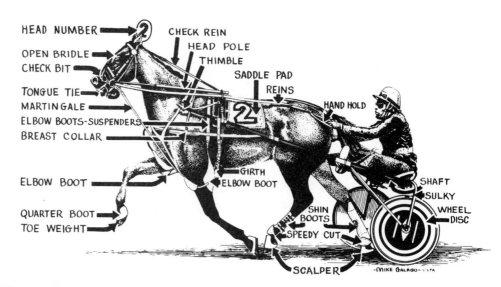

Ill. 9-7. *Equipment commonly worn by the trotter. (Artwork/Courtesy of the United States Trotting Assn.)*

Ill. 9-8. *Manners are important on a crowded track. (Photographer/George A. Smallsreed, Courtesy of the United States Trotting Assn.)*

two 24-inch rubber-tired, wire-spoked, metal-rimmed wheels. The driver sits on a single seat above a three-leaf spring. He puts his feet in stirrups, metal supports attached below the shafts just behind the crosspiece. A vinyl flap, called an apron, spans the distance between the seat and the crossbar. A dash is attached to the crossbar. The dash and the apron are supposed to prevent dust, mud, and dirt from flying into the driver's face, but drivers wear goggles or safety glasses as additional protection. Training carts are generally of the "drop-heel" type. Their shafts extend back, ending above the wheels, rather than curving in toward the seat. The well-balanced training cart is used for breaking and training. For racing, the horse is harnessed to a sulky. This is similar to a training cart but is lighter because the shafts usually are constructed of fiberglass. It is also shorter, and has a sparer undercarriage and a wider wheel track. The driver sits on a single seat positioned very close to the hindquarters of the horse. His feet rest in stirrups on the shafts on either side of the horse. These stirrups, unlike cart stirrups, raise the driver's feet higher than the shafts. Horse and driver are so close that the hind legs of the trotter or pacer move beneath the seat during rearward extensions. Plastic wheel discs cover the spokes so that the horse cannot catch a hoof in a wheel during the race.

Special Training

Standardbreds, destined for careers as race horses, often are started in harness near the end of their yearling year. This gives trainers time to prepare the horses to race in the spring of their two-year-old year. Initial training parallels some aspects of the program outlined in chapter 2. The horses are introduced to harness parts and ground-driving skills, but the pace is quicker; experienced harness trainers may be ready to hook after a bare two weeks of preparatory training. They have learned to judge when to take shortcuts and when to spend extra time. Prior to hooking, little emphasis is spent on bending or circling (long-lining). A drag or poles are seldom used. The advantage of a broad track and knowledgeable assistance makes it safe and sensible to hook youngsters directly to a training cart.

A race horse must never become bored with his work, so the trainer can't afford to dwell in one area for too long. Manners are important, but they are allowed to come about naturally. For instance, a horse is jogged off after the first hooking; walking and standing are expected only after he is relaxed and familiar with the equipment and routine.

Beginners are worked in the afternoon when the stable is quiet. They are kept in the center of the track so that if they suddenly shy to the right or left there is no danger of bumping into the rail. When a young horse wearing blinders veers and heads for the fence, the trainer never pulls on the outside line to turn the head away. He knows that a green horse is much more likely to run into an object he can't see. Instead, he turns the horse toward the object and guides him past it. Delvin Miller, in *Care and Training of the Trotter and Pacer*, says: "I never saw a colt yet that would run into a fence or anything else intentionally. If you will notice colts running loose in fields . . . they will run helter skelter toward a fence, but will always turn just before they get there."

A yearling or newly started horse begins a schedule of workouts six days a week. He is jogged (a slow steady trot; the speed of the jog is relative to the top speed of the horse) for one and a half miles per day and worked up to three-mile daily jogs over a period of a month. During this period the horse is expected to begin walking and standing; he may be hooked in the barn and driven to the track. If all goes according to plan, the horse is ready to begin training after five or six weeks of jogging.

Training is exercise that prepares the horse physically and mentally to race. Training miles are faster than jogging miles, but the speed is relative. Once training miles are commenced, "brushing" must be introduced. Brushing teaches the green horse to speed up rather than slow down at the end of a training mile. The horse is asked to increase speed just a few yards from the end of the mile. The rate is slightly faster than the speed of the training mile and is never at top speed for any distance. Young horses may be willing, but speed is rough on their physique and is emotionally exhausting as well. A training session should end before the youngster is fatigued. The horses are jogged three miles six days of the week for a month. On three of the days the horse is trained one mile after jogging. Jogging speed and training speed are progressively increased, but speeds are individual. The schedule for each horse will be different. Youthful awkwardness predisposes green horses to accident or injury if they are rushed to perform at speeds which they lack the balance to maintain.

Horses race in a counterclockwise direction, so they are generally worked the wrong way of the track and "turned" to train and brush. Early in training, to assure balance and straightness, horses are jogged in both directions. As soon as serious training begins, the training miles are run in the direction of the race.

Two or three months after the initial hooking, a new phase of training begins. If all has gone according to plan, the horse will have improved stamina, strength, and aerobic capacity. It is time to begin conditioning for bursts of speed. "Repeating" is the track term for the new schedule. It is a form of interval training, which requires more than one controlled speed workout separated by periods of partial recovery. The horse is not cooled out or allowed to relax. He is provided time to "catch his breath" while his body is kept warm. The idea behind this type of conditioning is to stimulate the horse to go beyond reliance on oxygen to fuel his energy demands. Instead, a biochemical change in response to stress releases energy stored in the muscles (similar to the change that occurs when a horse is frightened into flight). Interval training conditions the horse over a period of time to perform for gradually increasing lengths of time at speed. The pulse rate must be raised to between 180 and 220 beats

Ill. 9-9. The people involved with harness racing combine a love of horses and driving sport that has led them to accumulate a wealth of information on both subjects. (Photographer/George A. Smallsreed, Courtesy of the United States Trotting Assn.)

per minute. Usually three "trips" (speed workouts) separated by forty minutes after a recovery) are standard, working up from two. The individual horse must always be the guide. If the pulse during the last workout is higher than the previous two, or if it remains high during recovery periods, the horse is fatigued. The third trip is of no value to this horse. He should be dropped back to two trips. Two sessions of interval training, evenly spaced over the training week and separated by intervals of jogging, are maximum at any stage of training. Some trainers do go to four trips, a session prior to a race, but never more than two sessions per week. Since Standardbreds commonly race in heats (more than one race determines the winner), interval training is essential.

Schedules work wonders, but they must be flexible. A horse is never worked if he is sick or unsound, or if conditions are unsafe.

Speeds are progressively increased throughout all phases of race training. Although a horse may be willing and capable of producing, he is never asked for speed until he has the necessary muscling, endurance, and wind to sustain it. Rushing—asking too much too soon—is a mistake that often occurs when a trainer is pushing to prepare for a race or is eager to test the potential of a young horse. Rushing is considered the quickest way to spoil a race horse. The consequences can be physical and/or mental; in many instances they ultimately end the career of the horse. To be successful, trainers must be patient, staying within the bounds that prevent fatigue, boredom, and stress. In other words, winning the race isn't everything. Future soundness and healthy attitude have to be preserved for the long run.

The people involved with harness racing combine a love of horses with a love of driving sport, and their enthusiasm has led them to accumulate a wealth of information on both subjects. Even though an actual race is beyond the scope of most drivers, the lore and literature of the sport can apply to other areas and prove a valuable aid. It is easy to become insulated within a discipline, but active, open, exploratory minds are rewarded. And, because each specialty has at least one highly researched object of pursuit, the interchange is beneficial to both parties.

More information about harness racing can be obtained from the United States Trotting Association (see the Appendix).

10

COACHING, PARADES, STATE OCCASIONS

Literature has been a wonderful promoter of the romance and fantasy that flavors coaching tradition and history. Fairytale princesses and handsome nobility ride through the pages of stories and novels in coaches of glass or gold embellished with precious metals and glittering jewels. Invariably these privileged passengers are drawn to their destination by two or four refined, high-stepping white or gray horses. The royal family of England owns a golden coach, and the "grays" stabled in the Royal Mews are reserved for use only by the Queen and her immediate family. Contrast this real-life splendor with another scene: the dark coach that thunders through the predawn mist, drawn by a team of black horses who strike sparks from the stones beneath their hooves. A villain, perhaps Count Dracula, lurks with-

Ill. 10-1. C. W. Watson driving a coach and four at the New York State Fair in the early 1900s.

in the enclosed body of this vehicle. The symbolism of the dark coach also has a factual counterpart, in that black horses used to draw the hearse at many state and military funerals. (The U.S. Government will provide a black horse and funeral vehicle, if requested, for military funerals.)

Broadly defined, a coach is a four-wheeled vehicle that seats four passengers, features a raised coachman's seat, and generally has a roof and paneled sides. As a descriptive term, *coach* can be used to identify a variety of vehicles that served utilitarian needs of the general public, as well as the more esoteric requirements of the wealthy, for approximately four centuries. Road coaches, park drags or coaches, mail coaches, stagecoaches, broughams, coupes, rockaways, barouches, landaus, bretts, caleches, victorias, and state or dress chariots are some of the vehicles that can be united within the category of *coach*. However, under this definition there are vehicles that differ from one another in function and design, and some that offer exceptions to almost every point of the previous definition of a coach. For instance, broughams and coupes are called half-coaches because they have room for only two passengers. Landaus—for instance, the Ascot landau that traditionally carries the Queen of England around the track to open the racing season—usually are seen with tops folded down and do not always have a raised coachman's seat. A boxless coach can be postillion-driven; each pair of horses is handled by a rider who is seated on the nearside horse and leads the offside horse. He controls the ridden horse with a pair of ordinary riding reins and has a line attached to both sides of the bit of the other horse (Ill. 2–1).

The Hungarians are considered responsible for building the prototype of the modern coach, or "spring carriage," during the fourteenth century. A town in Hungary that may be the birthplace of the vehicle, or at least the area that witnessed its early use, is named Kotsee. Kotsee sounds very like coach when pronounced in English. The original coach differed from preceding vehicles in that it had a rudimentary system of springs from which the body hung by leather straps, above the undercarriage. It wasn't until the seventeenth century that the familiar carriage, with smaller front wheels to increase maneuverability and improved springing between the body and the framework, made an appearance.

The Italians took over where the Hungarians left off and were the first to use and produce coaches in any number during the sixteenth century. They built fabulous, ornate, heavy, open vehicles decorated with scrollwork and sculpture. In 1525 there were fifty coaches in use in Milan as compared to the three in use in Paris twenty-five years later. There is some disagreement regarding the appearance of the first coach in England. Some say Walter Rippon made a coach for the Earl of Rutland in 1555. Others believe the forerunner was imported from Holland by a Dutchman, William Boomer, for Queen Elizabeth I. It is known that the first state coach was made by Walter Rippon in 1571 and that coaches were being used routinely by the aristocracy as early as 1580.

Throughout the sixteenth and much of the seventeenth century the coach was considered an effeminate vehicle, suitable only for women. An edict published by Pope Pius IV advised that cardinals must maintain the dignity of the church and ride horses rather than travel in coaches. In 1601 a bill was introduced (though not passed) into the English Parliament that was intended to limit the use of coaches, which were seen as a threat to the art of horsemanship.

During the reign of Louis XIV, France gained leadership of the coaching industry. During the 1700s France was producing more carriages than any other country and continued to do so until the revolution. French coachbuilders became masters of elegant, flowing forms that masked the structural elements of the vehicles, and they made ornamentation become an end in itself. Their heavy, imposing vehicles were more truly works of art.

With the end of the Rococo period, the emphasis turned to practicality. Mechanically minded English coachmakers came into their own in the nineteenth century, and satisfied the demand for faster, lighter, more useful vehicles. The English produced a line of efficient, sporty vehicles that gained the respect of drivers worldwide; some are still in use today. The Italians developed the so-called European type of coach during this era. These were mostly variations of the "Berlin," a conservative, enclosed carriage that originated during the late eighteenth century in Germany. But there were also occasional fanciful creations for wealthy patrons, such as the Neo-Baroque parade coach of Ludwig II of Bavaria.

Both the utility and the glamour of coaching reached a highpoint during the nineteenth century. The period between 1815 and 1840 became known as "the golden age of coaching." Commercial coaches reached their peak of sophistication and efficiently moved mail, freight, and passengers. Coachmen indulged in coaching races, and reports state that some vehicles traveled as fast as 19 miles per hour although fines were imposed on reckless drivers. 10 mph was the scheduled speed. Private and state coaches, always elegant but displaying much variation, crowded the thoroughfares as transportation for the well-to-do and added formal emphasis to ceremonial occasions. Fashionable ladies drove well-bred, high-moving, and impeccably mannered horses through city parks on sunny summer afternoons. But the golden age was short-lived. After only twenty-five years the glory began to fade. Railroads began to erode coaching territory by acquiring the lion's share of passenger and freight business. The internal-combustion engine, with the advent of the twentieth century, dealt the finishing blow to commercial coaching.

Coaching Clubs

The romance and sport of private coaching were not easily extinguished, however. Coaching clubs sprang into existence in England and the United States during the latter half of the nineteenth century. Their aim was to preserve the spirit and the intricate, strict traditions of this specialty. The Coaching

Ill. 10-2. A victoria, an elegant and fashionable vehicle popular during the 1800s. It is four-wheeled, seats two adults, and has a facing hinged fold-away seat to seat two children. It resembles a phaeton, but is coachman-driven.

Club of England was founded in 1871 and has held at least two official meets each year since its inception (except during the two world wars). Membership is select and is limited to men. The number has never been allowed to exceed forty (its current membership). Members are elected, yet they may not publicly or privately seek election. To qualify, a candidate must be able to drive a four-in-hand to a coach. Coaching Club members wear a blue coat with brass buttons and a buff waistcoat. A cornflower displayed in the buttonhole is traditional. This dress is a tribute to the first president of the Coaching Club, the Duke of Beaufort, whose livery serves as its model. The present Duke of Beaufort is a member, as is the Duke of Edinburgh (Ill. 8-1). The Coaching Club supervises coaching classes at several major shows in England each year which are open to drivers other than Coaching Club members. Drivers are judged on the road during a marathon and in a show arena. A panel of twelve, appointed by the Coaching Club, determines awards. Appointments and turnout are taken into account and must be traditionally correct. Similar competitions are held in the United States during the Devon Horse Show (Devon, Pennsylvania) and in Canada at the Toronto Winter Fair.

Formal Processions

Coaches have remained popular throughout the world as a means for royalty and high government officials to dramatize the formality and ceremonial custom of state occasions. The Royal Mews at Buckingham Palace and Windsor Castle contain about eighteen gray carriage horses (used only by the royal family) and about twenty-four bay carriage horses for use by others. The Mews also shelter a collection of vehicles which includes the Gold Coach, five state coaches, ten state and semi-state landaus, five Ascot landaus, plus barouches and many other carriages and sporting vehicles. It is probably the largest collection of working carriages in the world. The Lord Mayor of London, the Speaker of the House of Commons, and a few peers maintain state or family coaches which they turn out for important events, such as a coronation or a royal wedding. Queen Elizabeth travels to the opening of Parliament in a carriage procession with an escort of Household Calvary. She rides in the Irish state coach which is drawn by four horses and driven from the box by the head coachman. The Queen meets visiting heads of state with a traveling landau to which are put six postillion horses. Other carriages and an escort accompany the Queen on these occasions. Carriages also are used for royal weddings, funerals, anniversaries, and other noteworthy ceremonies. The Gold Coach, drawn by eight postillion-ridden gray horses, is turned-out only for coronations. The business of state also requires ambassadors and their suites be taken in semi-state landaus, pulled by pairs of bay horses, to present their credentials. One or more broughams, drawn by a single horse, take official papers around London each day. The Duke of Edinburgh's competition horses are also part of the Royal Mews establishment. They are used for ceremonial occasions and royal processions as well as in competition.

Parades

Parades, a layman's counterpart to formal processions, are used to celebrate numerous occasions. The grand pageant of the Rose Parade in Pasadena that greets the New Year is one example, the opening-night festivities at a county fair, kicked off by a march down the main street of town, is another. Both types of parades commonly feature harness horses and often coach horses. Parade organizers offer awards for participants, who may register to compete in one of several categories. The harness division is usually called Horse Hitch. It draws a diverse group of entrants. A tiny pony put to a basket cart will compete with draft teams pulling farm wagons and/or a coach and four. Most parades seek sanction from a local, state, or national organization which standardizes rules, provides judges, and in some cases establishes a program of year-end awards.

Ill. 10-3. An antique pony wagon and team of ponies waiting to take part in the Swallows Day Parade, San Juan Capistrano, California. (Photographer/Joanne Feldman)

Parades usually have a theme—frontier days, Spanish southwestern, or Gay Nineties, for example—and competitive paraders plan their costumes and equipment to coincide with the theme. Parades are one type of driving competition where period costumes are expected, and these should be authentic, from hat to shoes, since they play an important part in the judge's decision.

Cleanliness of turnout is important. The horses should be sleek, fit, and groomed to perfection. In fact, since they are show horses, they should be presented with all the meticulous care outlined in chapter 6. The harness and vehicle must be immaculate and in a state of good repair. A parade judge is very particular. He or she may run a gloved finger over the harness, check a horse's tail for tangles, ask to see the shoes hidden beneath a long skirt, and shake a wheel to see if the axle is worn or the nut needs tightening.

Each division is prejudged at a specific time before the parade begins. This initial judging determines a major portion of an entrant's total score (usually 60 percent). Points are docked if a competitor is late. If the judge has finished prejudging or if time is short, he has the right to refuse to judge those who are late. Prejudging is similiar to presentation in combined driving. Each turnout is judged individually at the halt, although some judges will ask a competitor to perform a simple maneuver, such as walk/trot/halt, in order to gauge the skills of the driver.

Most parades take place on asphalt pavement, and special shoeing is required to ensure the safety of the horse. Refer to chapter 5, "Pleasure Driving," for more information on this subject.

Special training also may be necessary to prepare a horse for the stress of crowds, noisy bands, and the normal confusion of the paradegrounds and the parade itself. Some information on this subject is included later in this chapter. If you are bringing a green or novice horse to a parade, it is a good idea to mark this fact on your entry form. Most parade committees will assign a new horse a position in the lineup that is some distance from loud marching bands or other major distractions.

An additional 40 percent of the total score is determined during the parade as an entrant passes the reviewing stand. The judge usually is positioned on a raised platform and has a clear view of competitors as they approach, pass, and continue along the parade route. It is important to present a picture of competence and assurance as the vehicle passes the stand. Some riders perform a maneuver, such as a figure eight or a turn on the haunches, in front of the reviewing stand, a form of display that is not practical for the drivers of vehicles.

Be courteous when driving in a parade. Don't tailgate on the entry in front of you and don't lag to talk to friends on the sidelines, holding up the parade in back of you. Both these indiscretions will lower a judge's opinion of a competitor and may cause problems for other entrants. Also, you should wait until the entry preceding you has left the area in front of the reviewing stand before you enter it. Extend your courteous behavior to the awards ceremony; whatever your standing, take it with good grace. Most judges attend award presentations and make themselves available to competitors as a source of information to improve future performances. They are willing to explain, but *never to justify*, their decisions.

A more formal type of parade is called a "coaching meet." These were popular during the latter half of the nineteenth century, when groups of amateur drivers, often members of a coaching club, would gather for scenic drives. The Coaching Club of New York held annual midsummer meets during the height of the fashionable Newport, Rhode Island, "season." The highlight of these annual parades was a change of formation called, "the Maneuvre." One after the other, drivers pulled out of the line and drove to the front of the parade to salute the leader, who was also the president of the club. The driver then took a place in front of the leader and the procedure continued until each driver had changed position and the president was at the end of the line. At this point the president would pull out and drive past the entire line to again take his position at the head of the parade.

Coaching meets are again becoming popular. The Preservation Society of Newport County sponsored a summer weekend of coaching in 1982 in an attempt to revive the old tradition.

The Coach Horse

The coach horse is not a specific breed of horse, although some breeds were developed to be coach horses. Rather, it is a specific type of horse. Height is not a prerequisite for a coach horse (they average between 14.2 and 16.2 hands) except as it applies to the size of the vehicle. Still, because of the heavy work involved, coach horses are generally more substantial than light-harness horses. A coach horse should be attractive and strongly built and should display hardy spirit. Horses that are used with ornamental, formal, state, or semi-state coaches must also be well bred and exhibit an eye-catching way of moving. Morgan, Hackney, Friesian, and Cleveland Bay horses are examples of breeds that make excellent coach horses because they combine these characteristics. Morgan Horses are discussed in some detail in chapter 6, and brief descriptions of the other breeds follow. More information can be obtained by contacting the breed registries listed in the Appendix.

The Hackney Horse is a traditional coach horse (Ill. 1–6). It is an elegant animal known for round, showy action that is both elevated and ground-covering, a combination that makes the Hackney ideally suited to the pomp and ceremony associated with coaching. The breed was developed in England and is said to be decended from the Norfolk Trotter. The Hackney Horse Society was founded in 1883 and has maintained a stud book ever since. Queen Elizabeth was president of the Society during its centenary year, 1983. The Hackney Horse Society maintains a panel of about forty judges who officiate at their breed shows. Hackneys are shown in hand and in harness at about thirty British shows throughout the season. More than 500 registered Hackneys have been exported since 1961, most of them going to Holland, America, Australia, South Africa, Canada, and Italy.

The Friesian (Ills. 2–1, 7–1) is a coach horse native to the Netherlands. To be registered, individuals must be predominantly black; the only white permitted is a small star. Average height is over 15 hands. Considered the heaviest of light horses, they sport the feathered fetlocks otherwise characteristic of draft breeds. Friesians are close-coupled, substantial, and strong, and move with impressive high action. In the late nineteenth century there was great demand for these horses to pull funeral vehicles. London alone had a "black brigade" of about 700 Friesian stallions used for this purpose. In recent years several Friesians have been exported to the United States to be used as carriage horses.

Another excellent coach horse, and one of the oldest British breeds of horse, is the Cleveland Bay. Always bay color, these horses are strong and tractable. They are often crossed with other breeds and produce admirable offspring; an example is the Yorkshire Coach Horse, half thoroughbred, which was popular during the 1800s. The Duke of Edinburgh drives a four-in-hand of Cleveland Bays at combined driving events and British driving trials (Ill. 7–1).

A single coach horse, between 15.2 and 16.2 hands, can be expected to pull a vehicle weighing between 1,200 and 1,400 pounds. In fact, a conditioned horse can be expected to pull five or six times his own weight at a walk for several hours without undue stress. Lighter vehicles (using a ratio of weight to size as a guide) are suitable for smaller single horses; heavier equipages require pairs and teams. Distance and speed of travel also must be taken into consideration when determining how much weight a horse can comfortably pull.

The horse expends the most energy getting the vehicle in motion. Once the coach is moving, considerably less strength is required to keep it going forward. Of course, much depends on the going. An upgrade or downgrade requires more work on the part of the horse to keep the vehicle moving at an even pace. Also, the deep footing considered ideal for saddle horses adds to the difficulty of pulling a heavy vehicle. A firm base with a shallow, loose cushion (approximately 3 inches deep) is best for a driving horse. The width of the wheel rims and the condition as well as the type of tread determine traction and play a part in determining the difficulty of the pull. The angle of the shafts is another very important factor. Shafts are best positioned for pulling weight when they are lower than the horse's chest at an average oblique incline of 12 degrees. Lastly, the disposition of a horse affects his stamina; the nervous or fussy horse tires much sooner than the calm, steady worker.

A coach horse, like all competitive horses, must be prepared with painstaking year-round care for meets, parades, and ceremonial occasions. Proper nutrition, exercise, conditioning, and grooming is vital to optimum appearance and performance. Chapters 6 and 7 contain more information on these subjects.

Equipment

Coach harness is much the same as the standard harness for single and multiple horses. The formality of the coach determines to a large extent the style and ornamentation of the harness. For instance, a park drag needs a showy black harness with brass fittings; state equipages require harness of this quality but with the addition of elaborate family crests; road-coach harness, on the other hand, can be plain russet or black harness with russet collars. The style of bit must complement the harness. Dressy Buxton bits are correct with drags, semi-state, or state vehicles. Buxtons are similar to liverpools, but the cheekpieces are curved, and occasionally decorated with carving. Liverpools or elbow bits are correct with road coaches and other, less formal vehicles.

While the harness is fairly standard, the vehicles themselves offer plenty of variety. A popular form, the barouche, is a luxurious four-wheeled vehicle with a raised coachman's seat. Barouches are equipped with leather extension tops, but being summer vehicles, they have no sides. In dry weather

Ill. 10-4. A brougham.

the top is folded down and the vehicle is open. A barouche is a dignified vehicle for four passengers that requires showy, high-class horses to complete the turnout.

The brett is an American version of the British barouche in that it has four wheels, a shallow body, and two facing passenger seats to accommodate four people, though the springing is different and the vehicle not quite so elegant. This vehicle is also driven by a coachman and needs well-bred, spirited horses.

The brougham or coupe (the coupe is the American counterpart) is more accurately described as a half-coach. It is a small, closed vehicle with paneled sides and a hard top. Although it is four-wheeled, it seats only one or two people. The brougham is a gentleman's carriage, coachman-driven and usually pulled by a single horse.

Caleches are elegant four-wheeled town vehicles that seat four passengers. They feature a folding leather top, a paneled front with a window, and sides equipped with glass shutters. The sides and front are easily removed and then the vehicle resembles a barouche. Caleches have been called the first convertibles.

State or dress chariots are formal equipages that were used chiefly by the aristocracy. They have enclosed bodies, a hard roof, and four wheels. They are driven from a box seat, the frame of which is covered with a hammer cloth (an elaborately folded and decorated velvet cloth). The hammer cloth and the harness are heavily embellished with the family crest. A pair of bays is traditionally put to a chariot. The coachman wears state livery as does the footman. This dress calls for a black three-cornered hat decorated with red ostrich feathers, a white wig, a scarlet coat with gold buttons, scar-

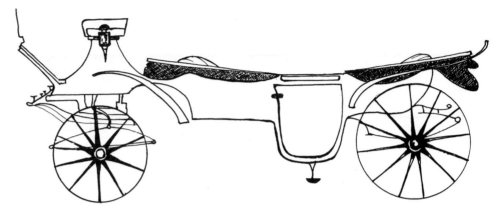

Ill. 10-5. A landau.

let knee breeches, pink silk stockings, black shoes with gold buckles, and white gloves.

The drag is a coach commonly used today because it is a sporting vehicle and can be owner- or amateur-driven. Its original design was based on that of the mail coach. It has four wheels, an enclosed body, and a raised coachman's seat. A drag can accommodate thirteen passengers plus two grooms and the driver. Four passengers can sit inside the vehicle, though rarely do except to take advantage of the convenience with which some were fitted, eight passengers share two roof seats, and one sits on the left of the driver. The two grooms share a rumble seat. Four high-moving and impressive horses are necessary to complete the turnout.

Landaus are fancy, four-wheeled carriages with deep, low bodies and two facing seats for four passengers. They are suitable for summer and winter because the top folds easily to turn a closed carriage into an open one. They can be driven from a raised coachman's seat or by postillion.

Mail coaches and stage coaches are large commercial, four-wheeled vehicles with solid sides, hard tops, and a coachman's box. Pulled by teams, they were used to transport passengers, parcels, mail, and other commodities until the railroads usurped their territory. These vehicles were strictly functional. The decorative harness and trim common to private coaches were never in evidence, and instead of grooms or a footman, they carried a guard. British stage coaches were in use by the 1600s. These were painted gray. British mail coaches were painted maroon and black with scarlet wheels and undercarriage. These were first used in 1784.

Road coaches are similar to drags, but they are public vehicles and so are less fussy in ornamentation. They came into use during the late nineteenth century as part of a carriage revival, serving the tourist business that remained after the railroads had driven the stage coaches out of business. They carried more passengers than a drag since grooms were not required, although a guard usually rode on the vehicle. And, unlike the somber and tasteful drag or private coach, the road coach often was painted bright colors and decorated with gold lettering. A four-in-hand is put to a road coach.

The rockaway is a four-wheeled vehicle of American design. It has a tall, square body, a hard top, and leather curtains or paneled sides. These vehicles accommodate four to six passengers. They differ from other coaches because the driver sits on the same level as the passengers and the roof extends forward to offer him some shelter.

These are just some of the vehicles that qualify as coaches. Perhaps they don't all strictly adhere to the definition of "coach," but each one does fulfill some part of the definition, and all deserve mention if we are to do justice to coaching variety.

Special Training

A potential coach horse is started in harness following a gradual, sensible program of training and conditioning such as the one outlined in chapter 3 and elaborated on in portions of chapters 5 through 9. Some additional training is necessary, however, to prepare these horses to be calm despite noisy roadside crowds and parade bands, slippery asphalt footing, and other unique aspects customary at processions of all types.

Exposure training can prepare a horse, by introducing him to the sights and sounds he will encounter during a parade, and convincing him that these things do not constitute a threat. The exposure should be gradual and requires forethought, patience, and sensitivity on the part of the driver/trainer. It can begin while the horse is in the stall or paddock. Simply play a radio nearby (be absolutely sure the horse can't reach the cord). Continue the desensitizing process by carrying a transistor radio in the vehicle during daily drives. Play a variety of music at different volumes. If the facility where the horse is stabled is equipped with a public address system, ask the management to play marching band music on one or two occasions while the horse is working. Hang paper streamers and balloons from fence rails and trees, strew wads of paper, styrofoam cups, and sheets of newspaper on the ground and drive the horse regularly among these distractions. Ask a group of friends to stand beside the track and whistle, wave newspapers, and clap as you drive past. The horse must also be exposed to motor vehicles and be willing to work quietly in proximity to them (see chapter 5). Only a few parades, for instance, the Swallows Day Parade in San Juan Capistrano, are strictly limited to equestrian motive power.

Gradually build intensity and be prepared to proceed slowly if the horse appears unnerved by his new environment. A coach horse must have faith in his driver as well as self-assurance to handle the extraordinary sights and sounds common to his job. As with all specialized training, the schedule of progress should be tailored to the individual. A comfortable, confident horse, who can perform the task at hand, is proof of success.

In conclusion, chapter 10 weaves the final threads into the tapestry of information that makes up this book. I hope by beginning with a broad view of the elements of driving and moving on to specialized areas of harness sport, I have been able to present aspects that apply to, enlarge, and further, every driver's personal aims while increasing awareness of the many routes to the common goal, thus proliferating that goal: namely, horses performing successfully in harness.

APPENDICES

Suggested Reading

Books

Breaking and Training the Driving Horse: Doris Ganton
Care and Training of the Trotter & Pacer: James C. Harrison (United States Trotting Assn.)
Competition Carriage Driving: HRH the Duke of Edinburgh
Conditioning to Win: Don M. Wagoner (Equine Research Publications)
The Coach Horse: Stanley M. Jepsen
Driving: Anne Norris and Caroline Douglas
The Driving Book: Major H. Faudel-Phillips
A Guide to Driving Horses: Sallie Walrond
The Harness Makers' Illustrated Manual: W. N. Fitz-Gerald
Harnessing Up: Anne Norris and Nancy Pethick
Heroes in Harness: Philip Weber and Stanley M. Jepsen
Hints on Driving: Captain G. Moreley Knight
Horses and Horsemanship Through the Ages: Luigi Gianoli
Horsemastership: Margaret Cabell Self
Horse & Rider: Alois Podhajsky
Horse Tack: Julie Richardson
Hunter Seat Equitation: George H. Morris
The Morgan Horse Handbook: Jeanne Mellin
On the Box Seat: Tom Ryder
The Restoration of Carriages: George L. Isles
Riding and Schooling the Western Performance Horse: G. F. Corley, DVM
Show Driving Explained: Marilyn Watney and William Kenward
Work Horse Handbook: Lynn R. Miller

Magazines

The Carriage Journal: Carriage Association of America, RD1, P.O. Box 115, Salem, NJ 08079, U.S.A.
The Driving Digest Magazine: Catherine Tyler, Brooklyn, CT, U.S.A.
Equus: Fleet St. Corp., Gaithersburg, MD, U.S.A.
Horse & Driving: Watnoughs Limited, Bradford, West Yorkshire, England

Breed Registries

Appaloosa Horse Club, Inc.
P.O. Box 8403
Moscow, ID 83843

Arabian Horse Registry of America
3435 South Yosemite St.
Denver, CO 80231

Cleveland Bay Horse Society of America
P.O. Box 182
Hopewell, NJ 08525

Cleveland Bay Society
York Livestock Centre
Murton, Yorkshire, England

American Connemara Society
Hoshiekon Farm R.D. 1
Goshen, CT 06756

English Connemara Society
The Quinta
Bently, Farnham, Surrey, England

American Hackney Horse Society
P.O. Box 174
Pittsfield, IL 62363

Hackney Horse Society
National Equestrian Centre
Kenilworth, Warwickshire, England

American Morgan Horse Association, Inc.
P.O. Box 1
Westmoreland, NY 13490

American Quarter Horse Association
2736 West Tenth
Amarillo, TX 79168

National Quarter Horse Registry
Box 247
Raywood, TX 77582

American Saddlebred Horse Association, Inc.
929 South Fourth
Louisville, KY 40203

Welsh Cob Society of America
400 Head of the Bay Rd.
Buzzards Bay, MA 02532

Welsh Pony and Cob Society
32 North Parade
Aberystwyth
Cardiganshire, England

Welsh Pony Society of America
P.O. Box 2977
Winchester, VA 22601

International and National Driving Organizations

American Driving Society
c/o Melinda Brooks
P.O. Box 1852
Lakeville, CT 06039

American Horse Shows Association, Inc.
598 Madison Ave.
New York, NY 10022

American Road Horse & Pony Association
300 South Chiles
Harrodsburg, KY 40330

Australia Driving Society
c/o G.H. Winzer
3/42 Greenware Rd.
Wollongong, 2500, Australia

British Driving Society
c/o Mrs. Phyllis Candler
10 Marley Ave.
New Milton, Hampshire, England

Canadian Carriage & Cutter Association
c/o McPaul
1831-42 St., S.E.
Calgary, Alberta, Canada T2B lCl

United States Trotting Association
750 Michigan Ave.
Columbus, OH 43215

Carriage Association of America
Box 3788
Portland, ME 04104

Combined Driving Committee
British Horse Society
National Equestrian Centre
Kenilworth, Warwickshire, England

Federation Equestre Internationale
P.O. Box CH-3000
Berne 32 Switzerland

International Trotting and Pacing Association
575 Broadway
Hanover, PA 17331

Carriage Makers, Harnessmakers, and Suppliers

(This list does not imply a recommendation by either the author or the publisher.)

A & D Buggy Shop (carriage restoration)
Route 5
Millersburg, OH 44654

Arrowhead Acres Tack & Harness (harness and vehicles)
R.F.D. #5 Middle Rd.
Preston, Norwich, CT 06360

G & A Bates (harness maker)
Church Walk
Telford, Shropshire, England

H. Belfield & Son Ltd. (wheelwright and vehicle restoration)
Rocks Mill, Smallbridge
Rochdale, Lancashire, England

California Carriage & Harness Co. (carriage builder, wheelwright, harness and equipment)
2909 Oregon Court C-4
Torrance, CA 90503

The Carriage House (vehicles and harness)
95 Main St.
East Hampton, CT 06424

Carriage Works (wheelwright, vehicle restoration, harness)
Box 11D
Oakland, OR 97462

Chick Harness & Supply, Inc. (racing and show carts, harness, etc.)
U.S. Rt. 13, P.O. Box 71
Harrington, DE 19952

Croford Coachbuilders Ltd.
Dover Place, Ashford, Kent, England

Enterprises (carriage manufacturer)
Saxley Hill Barn
Meath Green Lane
Horley, Surrey, England

Fenlands (trap and gig builders)
2 Station Rd.
Isleham, Ely Cambs CB7 5QT England

Frizzell Coach & Wheel Works (carriage builder, restorer, wheelwright, and harness maker)
P.O. Box 82001
Oklahoma City, OK 73148

Richard Gill & Sons Ltd. (carriage builders and restorers)
Brame Lane
Norwood, Harrogate
North Yorkshire, England

H.J. Griffiths (web harness maker)
Glanyrafon Est.
Aberystwyth, Dyfed, SY23 3HJ Wales, England

Alfred Hales (wheelwright and coach painter)
The Hackney Stables
Manor Rd., Wales
S31 8PD, Yorks, England

Have Mule Will Travel (wheelwright, coachbuilder, restorer)
Sky Mesa Ranch
P.O. Box 1082
Dept. DD
Alpine, CA 92001

Hostetler's Harness Shop (harness maker)
Rt. 1, Box 172 A
Arthur, IL 61911

J. A. Jacks & Son (vehicle manufacturer)
9 Heoly Dwr, Hay on Wye
Hereford, England

Kloter Farms Carriage Stop (vehicles and accessories)
Rt. 140
Ellington, CT 06029

Kromer's Carriage Shop (wheelwright, carriage builder and restorer)
RR #4, Box 115
Hodgenville, KY 42748

Martin Auctioneers, Inc. (carriage and equipment auctions)
P.O. Box 71
Blue Bell, PA 17506

Myopia Carriage Co. (competition vehicles)
107 Dodge St.
Beverly, MA 01915

C. J. Nicholson (carriage builder)
Sandy Close Farm
Sherfield English
Nr. Ramsey, Hants S05 0FW England

Old West Coach & Supply (restoration, wheelwright, supplies)
Box 64
Joliet, MT 59041

Ozark Manufacturing Co., Inc. (manufacturer of carts)
P.O. Box 2342
Joplin, MO 64801

Smuckers Harness Shop (harness makers)
R.D. 3
Narvon, PA 17555

Wagonland Barn (vehicles and harness)
South Street
Bernardston, MA 01337

Westby Carriage, Ltd. (competition and traditional vehicles)
Postal Drawer Y
Andover, NJ 07821

Wilform Buggy Works (racing and show carts; harness; repairs and restoration)
1322 Coronado Ave.
Long Beach, CA 90804

INDEX